an illustrated intrc

THE BATTLE OF BRITAIN

Henry Buckton

In this painting by Joe Crowfoot, entitled *Angry Skies*, a Spitfire of No. 19 Squadron shoots down a Messerschmitt Bf 109E during the Battle of Britain. (Copyright Joe Crowfoot)

First published 2015

Amberley Publishing
The Hill, Stroud
Gloucestershire, GL5 4EP

www.amberley-books.com

British Library Cataloguing in Publication Data.
A catalogue record for this book is available from the British Library.

ISBN 978 1 4456 4202 4 (paperback)
ISBN 978 1 4456 4210 9 (ebook)

Typesetting and Origination by Amberley Publishing.
Printed in Great Britain.

CONTENTS

"LET US GO FORWARD TOGETHER"

THE BATTLE OF BRITAIN
IN FIVE MINUTES

In the summer of 1940 the fate of Britain hung in the balance. Across the English Channel the Nazi hordes were massing, preparing to invade this green and pleasant land. With lightning speed and military brilliance they had already conquered all before them. Then, during the summer of 1940, Nazi Germany would suffer its first defeat in a desperate struggle in the sky over southern England that became known as 'The Battle of Britain'.

With regards to the battle, dates are a little ambiguous. Some German sources suggest that it began on 4 July, while others insist that it started on 13 August. In Britain 10 July is generally accepted as the starting point.

The battle had four distinct phases, the first of which began when the Germans concentrated their attacks largely on shipping in the English Channel. In some ways this was a continuation of the aerial and naval blockade of Britain that had been going on for some time, which the Germans called 'Kanalkampf', and, although an invasion seemed almost inevitable after France had signed an armistice with Germany on 22 June, many high ranking Nazis still thought the blockade was a better solution. By starving the nation through the disruption of its sea trade, perhaps the British would capitulate without a fight and the German leader, Adolf Hitler, could turn his attentions to Russia, which he considered to be a much more serious threat to his territorial ambitions in the east.

However, if an invasion was to be mounted, the Germans knew that this could only be achieved once they had gained air supremacy over the landing beaches. If they could eliminate the RAF's home defence force, Fighter Command, from the equation, their own Air Force, the Luftwaffe, would have free range to bombard any ships or coastal batteries that might oppose their troops as they came ashore. So by attacking convoys in the Channel, the Luftwaffe and its commander-in-chief, Reichsmarschall Hermann Göring, aimed to stretch Fighter Command's resources, test their strength, and hopefully reduce their numbers. After all, every British fighter shot down into the sea would be one fewer to face in the impending struggle. Equally important to the Germans was to disrupt the supply of things like coal and raw materials to British factories, particularly those which Lord Beaverbrook, the Minister of Aircraft Production, had promised would quickly replace every aircraft lost in combat.

The opening phase of the battle lasted until 13 August 1940, at which point the Germans changed their tactics; they stopped attacking convoys in the Channel and instead began a major assault against Fighter Command itself. Their new strategy was to attack all of the British airfields in the south-east of England, while at the same time destroying as many enemy aircraft as they could, both in the air and on the ground. By knocking out airfields and communications systems so that the RAF would be unable to use them, their thinking was that Fighter Command would be powerless to stop the German invasion fleet as it crossed the Channel. The Germans called this phase of the battle 'Adlerangriff', or Eagle Attack, and it began on 'Adlertag', Eagle Day. It was supposed to have lasted for five consecutive days, which according to Göring was all the Luftwaffe would need to complete the victory. However, bad weather and the bravery of the British pilots, whom the Prime Minister Winston Churchill named 'The Few', made this impossible.

During all stages of the battle the German bombers were escorted to their targets by fighter aircraft, most notably the Messerschmitt Bf 109E. It was their job to prevent any British combat planes from hindering the progress of the raid but, at the same time, to provoke them into combat in order to shoot down as many as possible before the invasion could begin. In the main, Fighter Command had two principal aircraft, the Hawker Hurricane, which normally attacked the bombers, and the Supermarine Spitfire, which tackled their escorts; the iconic image that perpetuates from the time is of Spitfires and Me 109s engaged in mortal combats over south-east England, known as 'dogfights.' Less romantic but equally important during the battle was the part played by RDF, an early radar system that alerted Fighter Command to each raid so that the enemy could be intercepted and dealt with.

During the battle, certain dates stand out in terms of their significance towards its final outcome. One of these was 15 August, which produced some of the hardest fighting of the entire period and the Luftwaffe's biggest single daily loss of aircraft. Consequently it became known as Black Thursday. 18 August was another such day, during which the Luftwaffe's Junkers Ju 87 dive-bomber, known as the 'Stuka', suffered so badly that it was withdrawn from the battle, not to be used again.

The third phase began on 24 August and saw a sharp rise in the number of missions flown each day over southern England. With intense activity and the use of far greater numbers of fighters than in previous engagements, Göring hoped to sweep the RAF out of the sky and finally win air supremacy.

Up until this point, because of Hitler's express orders, London had been untouched. However, during the evening of 24 August bombs were mistakenly dropped on the capital. The following day RAF Bomber Command retaliated and bombed Berlin. This would prove to have a profound consequence on the outcome of the battle.

The fourth and final phase began on 7 September, when the Germans changed tactics again and began the large-scale bombing of London, hoping that the British government would seek terms. This proved to be the turning point of the conflict and a grave error by Göring and Hitler. In discontinuing their attacks on Fighter Command just at the point at which they were almost beaten, the Germans gifted its commander-in-chief, Air Chief Marshal Sir Hugh Dowding, the time he needed to rebuild his airfields and re-supply them with aircraft and men. From this point onwards Fighter Command steadily grew in strength, whereas the Luftwaffe could only weaken after each raid.

To coincide with the day's activity, Home Forces, including the Home Guard, were mobilized because it was believed the invasion was imminent. Twelve hours later they were stood down again as the German fleet failed to make an appearance.

The pivotal day of the battle came on 15 September when the Germans made two massive raids on London, during which they hoped to provoke Fighter Command into an all-out duel between the combat aircraft on both sides. They were successful in this aim but came off the worst, and by the end of the day, which is now annually observed as 'Battle of Britain Day', the Luftwaffe was unable to carry out many further raids of such magnitude.

On 18 September Hitler was left with no choice but to cancel the invasion and all the troops that had gathered along the French coast were withdrawn, never to reassemble. Although the Battle of Britain officially lasted until 31 October 1940, effectively it had been won at this point and Britain remained unoccupied and able to provide a platform from which to defeat the Nazis in the coming years.

TIMELINE

1940

- **10 July**
  The battle opens when the Luftwaffe makes a large-scale attack on a convoy of ships passing through the English Channel and Fighter Command responds.

- **27 July**
  The Admiralty concedes that they no longer have control of the Straits of Dover during daylight hours.

- **31 July**
  Hitler informs his chiefs of staff that the invasion of England must be executed by 15 September.

- **7 August**
  A massive and devastating attack on convoy 'Peewit' convinces the Air Ministry that the battle is about to enter a new phase.

- **13 August**
  Eagle Day – the Luftwaffe launches a new phase of the battle and begins to attack Fighter Command's airfields and infrastructure.

- **15 August**
  Black Thursday – the Germans suffer their biggest daily loss of aircraft during the battle, with seventy-five downed.

- **16 August**
  Flight-Lieutenant James Nicholson of No. 249 Squadron wins Fighter Command's only Victoria Cross of the battle.

- **18 August**
  Due to severe losses the Stuka dive bomber is withdrawn from the battle. Hitler postpones the invasion until 17 September.

- **24 August**
  The third phase of the battle commences with the Germans employing a greater number of fighters than before in an all-out bid to win air supremacy. London is bombed by mistake.

- **25 August**
  RAF Bomber Command bombs Berlin in reprisal for the German attack on London.

● **29 August**
   General Kurt von Doring claims that the Luftwaffe has won unlimited fighter supremacy over England. Hitler announces that the invasion fleet will set sail on 20 September.

● **7 September**
   Large-scale bombing raids on London mark the opening day of the London Blitz. British Home Forces, including the Home Guard, are mobilised, expecting the invasion at any moment.

● **8 September**
   A national day of prayer called for by His Majesty King George VI. People pray all over the country to be saved from invasion.

● **15 September**
   Battle of Britain Day – The Luftwaffe makes two massive raids on London but is soundly beaten by large numbers of RAF fighters.

● **18 September**
   Hitler cancels the invasion of Britain and withdraws his troops from the Channel ports.

● **25 October**
   Italian aircraft take part in a raid on Harwich.

● **31 October**
   Official end of the battle.

"NEVER WAS SO MUCH OWED BY SO MANY TO SO FEW"

THE PRIME MINISTER

1
SETTING THE SCENE

In some ways the Battle of Britain, or at least the prelude to it, began at the very start of the Second World War. After Britain and France had declared war on Germany in September 1939, the Nazis realised that in order to win the war they would probably have to invade both of these countries. German aircraft therefore appeared regularly in the sky over Britain, mainly engaged in photographic reconnaissance missions, taking photographs of things such as military installations, coastal defences, factories producing equipment for the war effort and transport systems. All of this would help them to draw up a picture of Britain's ability to defend itself against an invasion.

PRELUDE TO THE BATTLE

The first German incursion of any particular note into British airspace happened on 16 October 1939, when a group of Junkers 88s attacked ships of the Royal Navy anchored at Rosyth in the Firth of Forth. This resulted in the first two German aircraft being shot down over Britain during the war, both of which fell into the North Sea.

The first of these aircraft was claimed by Flight Lieutenant 'Patsy' Gifford of No. 603 (City of Edinburgh) Squadron, in Spitfire XT-A, based at the RAF airfield at Turnhouse. The second was claimed a few minutes later by Flight Lieutenant George Pinkerton of No. 602 (City of Glasgow) Squadron, flying out of RAF Drem. Remarkably, both of these pilots, and indeed the squadrons to which they belonged, were part of the Auxiliary Air Force, which had only recently been mobilised into full-time service. A few weeks prior to this, one had been a solicitor and the other a farmer.

Opposite: Popular wartime poster depicting pilots of Fighter Command during the Battle of Britain, accompanied by the words of Winston Churchill when he labelled them 'The Few'. (Copyright Muffinn and licensed for reuse under the Creative Commons Licence)

A Junkers Ju 88, the type of aircraft used during the first air raid on mainland Britain, is seen on a French airfield with aircrew.

Twelve days later, Flying Officer Archie McKellar, also of No. 602 Squadron, brought down the first enemy aircraft on to the soil of mainland Britain. The Heinkel He 111 made impact near Gifford, in East Lothian.

The first aircraft to fall on English soil was another Heinkel He 111, shot down near Whitby on 3 February 1940 by Hurricanes of No. 43 Squadron led by Squadron Leader Peter Townsend. By the summer of 1940, the sight and sound of German intruders in British skies was certainly nothing new.

GERMANY'S INVASION PLANS

By the end of June 1940 Germany had successfully invaded much of France, forcing the French to sign an armistice. This meant that Britain would now be fighting alone. On 2 July Adolf Hitler ordered his military chiefs of staff to draw up plans for the invasion of England, which within two weeks had been formalized; his intention to invade Russia was postponed until the following year. He did not wish to fight a war on two fronts and considered Britain to be the easier option. If he could quickly defeat the British and occupy their islands he would then be in a position to turn his full force against the Soviet Union, as he wished to secure huge territories for German resettlement in Eastern Europe.

The commanders of the German Army, who were in a buoyant mood after their recent military successes, agreed that an invasion that summer was a possibility. But Grand-Admiral Raeder, commander-in-chief of the German Navy, was a little more pessimistic, insisting that he would need more time to assemble enough boats. The truth was that Germany did not possess a fleet at that time that was capable of making a seaborne assault against the British coastline. In order to do this they began to assemble barges in ports along the French coast, many of which had previously been used on the Rhine or other rivers for freight transportation and were certainly not ideal.

But before the German navy could actually land its army on the beaches of Britain, its Air Force, called the Luftwaffe, would have to defeat the British Air Force to prevent it from hindering the operation. The head of the Luftwaffe, Reichsmarschall Hermann Göring, arrogantly boasted that his air fleet would be able to defeat the Royal Air Force within days of the start of the battle. Hitler was pleased and ordered that the attack on the RAF should begin at once, with the invasion being launched immediately after victory in the air had been secured.

THE AIR DEFENCE OF GREAT BRITAIN

On the other side of the English Channel, the part of the Royal Air Force that had the responsibility for defending the British coastline against the Luftwaffe was called Fighter Command. It was led by Air Chief Marshal Sir Hugh Dowding, mainly based at his administrative headquarters at RAF Bentley Priory, Stanmore, in Middlesex.

In order to defend Britain, the RAF divided the country into four parts, each of which was guarded by a Fighter Command Group. No. 10 Group, commanded by Air Vice-Marshal Sir Quintin Brand, covered South Wales and the west of England, from Land's End to Middle Wallop. No. 11 Group, under Air Vice-Marshal Keith Park, covered the south and south-east of England and encompassed the city of London. No. 12 Group, commanded by Air Vice-Marshal Trafford Leigh-Mallory, looked after the industrial Midlands and the remainder of Wales, reaching as far south as Duxford. And finally, No. 13 Group, under Air Vice-Marshal Richard Saul, covered Scotland and the north of England. But

Map showing the areas protected by the four Fighter Command groups. (Copyright Henry Buckton)

13 GROUP

Kenton Bar ●
● NEWCASTLE-
UPON-TYNE

● MANCHESTER

● RAF Watnall

12 GROUP

10 GROUP

RAF
Box

11 GROUP

RAF Uxbridge
● ●

● ●
BATH

LONDON

it was No. 11 Group that would bear the brunt of the majority of enemy raids throughout the battle, and it was here that the battle would be won or lost.

Although overall command of the battle was controlled from Bentley Priory, each of the four groups had its own headquarters: No. 10 Group at RAF Box in Wiltshire; No. 11 Group at RAF Uxbridge in west London; No. 12 Group at RAF

THE MEN IN CHARGE OF BRITAIN'S DEFENCE

Fighter Command itself was only one part in a wider organisation of home defence that began at the very top with the Prime Minister, Winston Churchill, whose war cabinet consisted of naval, military and air advisors, as well as the service chiefs of staff. The First Lord of the Admiralty was A. V. Alexander, and beneath him was the First Sea Lord, Admiral Sir Dudley Pound. Their responsibility was divided between the Home Fleet, Rosyth Command, Dover Command, Portsmouth Command and Western Approaches Command.

At the head of the War Office was the Secretary of State for War, Anthony Eden, and beneath him was the Chief of the Imperial General Staff, Field-Marshal Sir John Dill. They were in charge of all ground troops employed in the defence of the United Kingdom and their authority was divided between Home Forces and Anti-Aircraft Command. Home Forces itself, under General Sir Alan Brooke, was split into Scottish Command, Northern Command, Eastern Command, Southern Command, and Western Command. It would be the troops in these areas that would have the job of repelling the invasion, if it came.

The Air Ministry in July 1940 was headed by the Secretary of State for Air, Sir Archibald Sinclair, and beneath him was the Chief of the Air Staff, Air Chief Marshal Sir Cyril Newall. The Air Ministry had three branches, Bomber Command, under Air Chief Marshal Sir Charles Portal; Coastal Command, under Air Chief Marshal Sir Frederick Bowhill; and Fighter Command, under Air Chief Marshal Sir Hugh Dowding. As well as the previously mentioned four groups, Fighter Command also had responsibility for Balloon Command, under Air Vice-Marshal Owen Tudor Boyd; the Observer Corps, under Air Commodore Alfred Warrington-Morris; and joint command with the War Office for Anti-Aircraft Command, under Lieutenant-General Sir Frederick Pile. These collectively were the senior figures responsible for the defence of the nation at one of the most critical times in its recent history.

Watnall in Nottinghamshire; and No. 13 Group at Kenton Bar in Newcastle-upon-Tyne. And similarly, RAF Uxbridge in No. 11 Group would prove to be the busiest.

Each Fighter Command group was further sub-divided into smaller commands called sectors. Each sector station would alert a number of fighter bases of enemy incursions, enabling them to scramble their squadrons to intercept the enemy. No. 10 Group had sector stations at Filton and Middle Wallop; No. 11 Group at Biggin Hill, Debden, Hornchurch, Kenley, Northolt, North Weald and Tangmere; No. 12 Group at Church Fenton, Digby, Duxford, Kirton-in-Lindsey and Wittering; and No. 13 Group at Acklington, Dyce, Turnhouse, Usworth and Wick.

How Fighter Command Operated

As Fighter Command overall HQ, Bentley Priory had an operations room, where Hugh Dowding could see at a glance what was going on and where. It also

A Spitfire in the grounds of Bentley Priory, which was employed as Fighter Command headquarters during the battle. (Courtesy of John Murphy)

contained the Air Defence of Great Britain filter room. Here, information was received from the various elements of the warning system and filtered to remove duplication, doubt and confusion.

The operations room had a large plotting table with a map of the entire United Kingdom displayed on it. The filtered information was subsequently used to illustrate on this map where incursions were taking place. The information would also be forwarded to the relevant group operations room. For instance, if a raid was coming towards the south-east, RAF Uxbridge would be notified; if it was the north-east, Kenton Bar would be informed.

Each group HQ also had an operations room with a similar plotting table that showed a map of the area covered by the group and a significant part of its adjacent groups. This was just in case their own aircraft had to be vectored into another group's airspace on request from the CO of that group. This would happen most specifically later in the battle, when Keith Park found himself stretched in No. 11 Group and called on Quintin Brand at No. 10 Group and Leigh-Mallory at No. 12 Group for reinforcements. So although their aircraft were venturing into No. 11 Group's territory, they could still be directed from their own group headquarters. Each operations room also had a tote board that displayed the precise state of readiness of the fighter squadrons sector by sector. But without doubt the main operations room and nerve centre during the battle was at Uxbridge.

JOB OF THE SECTOR CONTROLLER

Each sector operations room was presided over by a controller. In front of him would also be a large plotting table with an outlined map of his sector of Britain, which, similar to the group operations room tables, would illustrate a significant part of the surrounding sectors. Information received from the various elements of the early warning system would be displayed on the operations room table by means of various symbols. Around the table sat ladies of the Women's Auxiliary Air Force (WAAFs), called plotters, who would record the movements of all aircraft in the area. Hostile or unidentified aircraft would be represented by yellow plaques with black numbers on them. These would be pushed around the map with plotting sticks.

The controller himself would usually sit in a gallery overlooking the table and next to him would be the Ops B officer, who manned a telephone switchboard connected to squadron dispersal points, adjacent fighter sectors and the Observer

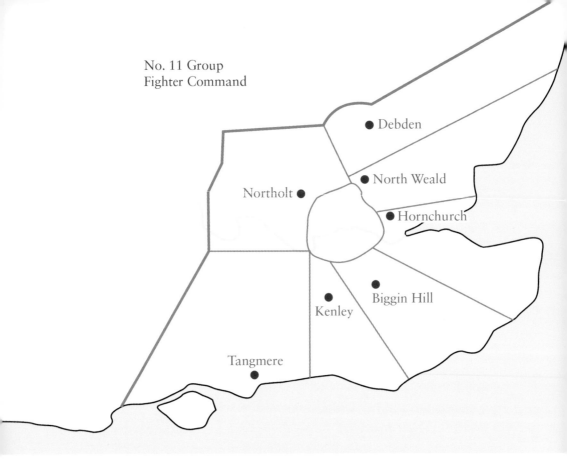

No. 11 Group
Fighter Command

Debden

North Weald

Northolt

Hornchurch

Biggin Hill

Kenley

Tangmere

This map shows how each Fighter Command Group was divided up into sectors. Here we see the sectors within No. 11 Group, which were responsible for the defence of the south-east corner of England, including London. (Copyright Henry Buckton)

Corps. Also in the gallery would be Ops A, usually a headphoned WAAF permanently connected to group headquarters. There would also be an Army Gun Liaison Officer who controlled the response of the sector's anti-aircraft defences.

So by July 1940, a sector controller was thus able to build up a complete picture of the progress of any aerial raid against his corner of Britain and would also be able to see the condition and availability of the fighter squadrons within his sector. He would know exactly their state of readiness and, if a squadron was in the air, he would be immediately aware of its location. In this way he would be able to conduct the movements of all his available aircraft against the raiders. He would also have information concerning the weather and cloud conditions readily at hand.

RADIO DIRECTION FINDING

In this way, Bentley Priory group and sector control rooms built up a picture of each raid as it happened. But where did the information come from that enabled them to do this? The fact was that by the start of the battle, Britain had in place the most comprehensive early warning system in the world, central to which was Radio Direction Finding, or RDF, later known as radar. RDF made it possible to detect an aircraft up to 100 miles away.

Many names are associated with the development of RDF, perhaps most surprisingly that of Air Chief Marshal Dowding himself, who before the war had been Air Member for Research and Development. In 1940, as head of Fighter Command, he must have been very thankful for having put his own faith in this infant initiative.

But how had radar come about in the first place? Worried by Germany's intense programme of aircraft development, particularly in the field of bombers, a group of scientists were appointed by the government before the war to set up an Aeronautical Research Committee to consider the best way of repelling an air attack. One of the possibilities they explored was the use of a death ray that had the ability to destroy approaching aircraft. When this idea was presented to Robert Watson-Watt of the radio department of the National Physical Laboratory, he regarded the concept itself as nonsensical, although on further consideration he admitted that it did have some consequential merit. For some time he had been working on a project for the Meteorological Office to measure the distance from the earth of the ionosphere by using radio waves. Employing a similar technique he found that radio signals bounced back from approaching aircraft, a discovery that ultimately led to the invention of RDF. On 26 February 1935, Dowding was invited to a demonstration given by Watson-Watt, in which he used the BBC's transmitter at Daventry to locate and track a Heyford aircraft. Dowding was suitably impressed and the money was provided to establish an experimental station at Orford Ness in Suffolk.

Although RDF made it possible to detect the presence of an aircraft from up to 100 miles away, it was unable to identify the type of machine. Nevertheless, this detection system could be used to warn Fighter Command about the potential threat of hostile aircraft.

Chain Home Radar mast at the site of the former RAF Stenigot in Lincolnshire. (Copyright J. Hannan-Briggs and licensed for reuse under the Creative Commons Licence)

CHAIN HOME AND CHAIN HOME LOW

By the start of the battle a number of RDF stations had been built all around the coast and were divided into Chain Home stations, which could detect aircraft flying at considerable height, and Chain Home Low stations, providing low-level raid cover. Although something of a secret weapon, the Germans certainly knew about the stations; in fact, this was unavoidable, as the Chain Home variants could be identified by their lofty towers, some of which were even visible from the French coast. It is also known that prior to the outbreak of war the Germans flew several reconnaissance missions to photograph and take a closer look at these towers. However, it is quite probable that, even right up until the start of the Battle of Britain, they did not quite appreciate their significance and thought that their purpose was more to do with the movement of enemy shipping rather than aircraft. This was probably due to the fact that the Germans had been developing their own system of radar, which was used solely for shipping purposes. Those that did recognise their aeronautical implications probably dismissed their accuracy and effectiveness.

Each RDF station had a powerful transmitter mast 360 feet high that sent out radio waves. These were bounced back from aircraft in flight and were received by a 240-foot receiver tower, which was linked to a cathode-ray screen in the hut below on which a recording of the reflected wave, or echo, was displayed as a

In terms of the south-west of England and South Wales, RAF Exeter was one of the most important airfields defending this general area. This memorial at Exeter airport, which now occupies the site of the old RAF station, was unveiled in March 2012 and is a tribute to all those who served here. (Copyright Henry Buckton)

blip and read by WAAF operators. Of course one of the beauties of this system is that it worked by day or night, and even during spells of inclement weather.

Throughout the summer of 1940 all RDF tracks would be communicated to the operations room at Bentley Priory, where this information was filtered and the relevant group headquarters notified. After that, other than taking responsibility for the ordering of public air-raid warnings, Fighter Command HQ took no further part in the daily battles. This responsibility fell on group HQs, most particularly, as already emphasised, Keith Park's No. 11 Group at Uxbridge, who would decide which sectors were best suited to deal with each impending emergency.

The fact that the RDF system had no way of distinguishing between friendly or hostile aircraft led to the invention of IFF (Identification Friend or Foe), where a small transponder was fitted to British fighters that presented a distinctive shape to the blip appearing on the cathode-ray screen. This enabled the operators to identify the aircraft as being friendly. Another device was called 'Pipsqueak'. This was fitted to aircraft radio telephones and periodically emitted a signal. It was very useful when trying to plot the course of an aircraft, especially when attempting to make night interceptions. And of course, if an aeroplane became lost for any reason, it was a means of guiding it home.

THE OBSERVER CORPS

Because of this RDF chain, hardly a German aircraft could cross the British coastline by day or night without being detected. The downside was that RDF could not monitor the progress of an aircraft once it was over land, so from the moment it crossed the coast the second part of the reporting system kicked in. This was the Observer Corps, an incredibly complex web of watching posts where observers waited at hilltop locations. As soon as an aircraft came into view and was identified as an enemy, the observation post would report its height, direction, nationality and type to an Observer Corps area centre via its direct landline. In turn, the area centre would pass the necessary information to a Fighter Command sector operations room. Sector would then process this information to alert the various parts of the defence system.

All the observation posts were built on high ground, from where their occupants commanded uninterrupted views. As well as knowing how to recognise both enemy and friendly aircraft by sight, observers also learnt how to distinguish between engine sounds. This was particularly useful at night, as observations had

The remains of a Second World War Observer Corps post near Chard in Somerset. (Copyright Henry Buckton)

to be maintained around the clock. Whether or not the identification of aircraft by sound alone was reliable remains a bone of contention. But in fact, as the Germans did not synchronise the engines of their multi-engined aircraft in the same way that the British did, their tone gave the trained ear a distinctive clue.

A field post was normally manned by two observers, who at this point in the war were mainly part-time volunteers. One of the two would report the movements of aircraft by telephone to their area centre, while the other operated the post plotter, which stood on a tripod in the centre of the post. This piece of equipment provided vital intelligence about the intruders and the following would be a typical message sent from a post observer to his area centre: 'Twenty He 111s approaching Winchester at 15,000 feet, flying north-west'.

Having noted the presence of an enemy aircraft, the observation post would maintain its reporting of it until it was out of sight. By this time the area centre would already be receiving information about the aeroplane from the next post on its flight path. At the area centre the messages sent by the posts were received by men and women called plotters, who sat around a large map table.

The map was sub-divided into hundreds of small numbered squares. Having received a report from a post, the plotter would place a coloured counter on to the appropriate square. As the reports progressed, following the course of the intruder, the plotter would move the counter from square to square, until such time as it left the area completely or was shot down. Above the plotters on a raised platform sat another group, called tellers, who had a comprehensive view of the situation from their elevated position. It was their job to report the movements of all aircraft to Fighter Command sector control rooms in order for them to scramble the necessary fighters.

So by 10 July, as the fate of Britain hung in the balance, the various elements of the early warning system detected and monitored every aircraft that crossed the coast, enabling the squadrons of Fighter Command to intercept and hopefully destroy them. For their work during the Battle of Britain the Observer Corps were later awarded a 'Royal' prefix.

A Hurricane of No. 85 Squadron is pictured here, flying over the English countryside. (Copyright Joe Crowfoot)

2
OPPOSING FORCES

In order to win air supremacy over Britain the timing may well have seemed perfect to the Luftwaffe, as the RAF had lost around 900 aircraft from all commands during the ill-fated campaign in France and Belgium. Having suffered so catastrophically, would Fighter Command be able to mount a coherent defence of Britain and would the British pilots have the stomach for more fighting following their recent defeat? These were the questions on the lips of many German airmen who were eager to bring their juggernaut to Britain.

Luftwaffe armourers preparing to arm a Me 110 before a mission over England.

THE RIGHT MAN FOR THE JOB

In order to defend Britain, Hugh Dowding calculated that he would need a bare minimum of fifty-four fighter squadrons. But after much of his force had been sent to France and Belgium, on 15 May he made a desperate appeal before Churchill's war cabinet explaining that if the home defence force was drained away, 'defeat in France would involve the final, complete and irremediable defeat of Britain'. Churchill considered his view and three days later ordered that no more fighters should go to France.

In political terms, if ever the right man was in the right place at the right time, it was Winston Churchill, who had only become Prime Minister on 10 May. Quite possibly, had Neville Chamberlain or some other premier still resided at 10 Downing Street, the British might have sought terms with the Nazis, perhaps even allowed a non-opposed occupation.

MINISTRY OF AIRCRAFT PRODUCTION

When he became Prime Minister, one of the first things Churchill did was to create a new Ministry of Aircraft Production, and on 14 May Lord Beaverbrook, the Canadian-born newspaper tycoon, was appointed its first minister. Beaverbrook was another 'man of the moment' who played an essential role in Fighter Command's victory. Under his directorship Britain's aircraft industry began to make up the losses suffered in France. But as well as motivating factories into producing more aircraft, he provided for the establishment of a network of maintenance and repair units. At these, battle-damaged fighters that could not be fixed by their ground crew were collected and made ready to go back into action again, using parts salvaged from other irreparable aircraft.

Lord Beaverbrook's media empire was based around the *Daily Express*, but as Churchill's Minister of Aircraft Production he used his entrepreneurial skills to great effect to galvanize the aircraft industry. In May, he managed to have 325 new fighter aircraft built, and in June, another 446. But production continued throughout the Battle of Britain, with 496 completed in July and 476 in August. Although unromantic and non-heroic, Beaverbrook's contribution to Fighter Command's victory is incalculable.

THE FEW

On the afternoon of 20 August 1940, Winston Churchill gave the House of Commons a speech on the progress of the war which included the following sentence:

> The gratitude of every home in our island, in our Empire and indeed throughout the world, except in the abodes of the guilty, goes out to the British airmen, who, undaunted by odds, unwearied in their constant challenge and mortal danger, are turning the tide of world war by their prowess and by their devotion. Never in the field of human conflict was so much owed by so many to so few.

This speech was made roughly halfway through the Battle of Britain but for the first time, at least in public, Churchill had referred to the airmen of Fighter Command as 'The Few', and a legend was born.

But who were the men that saved Britain from being occupied by one of the greatest armies ever created? The group of men Winston Churchill labelled 'The Few' were a varied bunch of individuals, officially totalling 2,927. These were the aircrew of Fighter Command and the Fleet Air Arm who prevented the Luftwaffe from winning air supremacy over the British Isles in the summer of 1940. Of these, 2,353 were British, but also within their ranks were Australians, New Zealanders, Canadians, South Africans, Southern Rhodesians, Irish, Americans, Polish, Czechoslovakians, Belgians, Free French, a Jamaican and even one Palestinian.

Some of these men were regular RAF who had joined the peacetime service between the wars, while others had enlisted at the onset. Some were members of the Auxiliary Air Force or Royal Air Force Volunteer Reserve, who had trained in the evenings and at weekends while at the same time holding down civilian jobs. Not all of them were officers, as some were recruited from the ranks to become senior NCOs. And they were not all pilots either, as their number also included wireless operators and air gunners. By the end of the battle itself, 544 had been killed.

HURRICANES AND SPITFIRES

Having established that 'the Few' were the airmen who fought and won the Battle of Britain, what about the weapons they used to secure their victory? The aircraft that did most damage to Germany's air fleets was the Hawker Hurricane, or 'Hurry', as it was sometimes called. It was designed by Sydney Camm and the prototype first flew on 6 November 1935. The Mark I had a maximum speed

Detail from a window in the priory church of St Mary and St Blaise at Boxgrove dedicated to Billy Fiske, who was one of a number of Americans who served with Fighter Command during the Battle of Britain. He was killed while serving at Tangmere in August 1940 and his grave can be found in the priory graveyard. (Copyright Henry Buckton)

Warhorse of the Battle of Britain: a Hawker Hurricane visits the former site of RAF Exeter in May 2012. (Copyright Brian Turnham and licensed for reuse under the Creative Commons Licence)

A Spitfire in Battle of Britain colours is here seen visiting the Goodwood motor racing circuit in 2010, which during the war was the site of a Fighter Command airfield. (Copyright Christine Matthews and licensed for reuse under the Creative Commons Licence)

of 325 mph. It was powered by a Rolls-Royce Merlin engine and normally carried eight .303 inch Browning machine guns. One important advantage that the Hurricane had over German fighters was its sturdiness. It had the ability to withstand a lot of battle damage and still keep flying.

The Supermarine Spitfire, on the other hand, was a development of the Schneider Trophy-winning seaplanes designed by R. J. Mitchell between the wars. Similar to the Hurricane, the Mark I was powered by the Merlin engine. It was armed with four .303 inch Brownings and had a maximum speed of 346 mph.

When large-scale formations began to attack Britain in the summer of 1940, as a general rule, the Hurricane squadrons were tasked with attacking the bombers, while the faster Spitfires were given the job of dealing with their fighter escorts.

OTHER AIRCRAFT AVAILABLE TO FIGHTER COMMAND

Fighter Command could also call on other aircraft, such as the Bristol Blenheim. This was the first aircraft to be fitted with a rudimentary form of airborne radar, which made the Blenheim squadrons the backbone of Dowding's night interception force, until they were replaced by the Beaufighter in mid September. But with only nine squadrons available to cover the whole of Britain, night interceptions were woefully inadequate.

Another aircraft used by Fighter Command was the Boulton Paul Defiant, a two-seater fighter. Its four machine guns were all situated in the dorsal turret, which meant that it could not fire forwards. Once the Germans had identified this handicap, it became easy prey to either a head on attack, or an assault from below.

The Gloster Gladiator was an out-dated biplane, but it could land on a much shorter runway than the monoplane fighters. For this reason it was used in the defence of the naval bases around Plymouth.

As for the two Fleet Air Arm squadrons under Dowding's command, they flew a variety of aircraft during the battle, including the Grumman Martlet, the Buffalo Mark I, and the Fairey Fulmar.

BARRAGE BALLOONS AND ANTI-AIRCRAFT GUNS

During the battle, as well as fighter aircraft, Dowding had other weapons in his arsenal that proved deadly to the Luftwaffe, such as barrage balloons. Britain's balloon barrage effectively prevented the Germans from making low-level bombing raids over vulnerable areas, because they forced them to fly at heights at which anti-aircraft guns and fighter aircraft could engage them. Each balloon was attached to a winch, usually on a lorry, by a thick steel cable, which proved lethal to any aircraft that flew into it.

The balloons were tethered in line about 100 yards apart, at heights up to several thousand feet, which meant that an enemy bomber flying at speed below the barrage had about a three-to-one chance of crashing into a cable. Once the pilot was forced to fly above the balloons he would come into range of the searchlights and so be a target for the ground defences.

The balloon barrages were operated by men or women of the Auxiliary Air Force and covered not only London but other vulnerable areas in the provinces, particularly industrial and shipping centres. A barrage balloon was also mobile, and could easily be moved from one location to another.

The anti-aircraft batteries in the British Isles also played a much greater role than they are often given credit for. In the twelve months ending on 31 December 1940, they shot down a total of 444½ enemy aircraft. The odd half represents the AA gunner's share in an enemy bomber that was finished off by RAF fighters after it had been winged by a near miss from a ground battery.

A 3.7 inch anti-aircraft gun on Clarence Esplanade, Portsmouth. This type of gun was effective against enemy aircraft to a range of up to 32,000 feet. (Copyright Henry Buckton)

THE ROYAL NAVY – THE UNKNOWN ENTITY

Often overlooked by historians during the course of the battle is the presence of the Royal Navy, which at that time was still regarded as one of the most powerful in the world, eminently more so than Germany's. With air superiority the Luftwaffe would be able to attack any British ships that put up resistance to the invasion, so part of Göring's battle strategy was to destroy the Royal Navy in their places of anchorage, by frequently bombing places such as Portland, Plymouth, Portsmouth and Rosyth and attacking any ships that moved within the Channel.

The Royal Navy will always therefore remain the unknown entity, as the invasion did not come to fruition. By then 'the Few' had already seized the day and halted Germany's advance.

THE STATE OF THE GERMAN AIR FORCE (LUFTWAFFE)

As it prepared to do battle over England, what did the Luftwaffe have in its favour? Most importantly, it had more aircraft than its enemy, by a ratio of approximately five to one. It also had more experienced pilots who had already seen action in several campaigns stretching from Spain to Norway. These pilots were full of confidence, and why not? So far they had defeated everyone before them, including the British Expeditionary Force in France.

But the Luftwaffe's strategy had been hurriedly conceived, literally thrown together in a few weeks, to accommodate Hitler's changing moods. The RAF's defensive strategy, on the other hand, had been etched out and tested for at least the previous four years.

HERMANN GÖRING (GOERING) THE REICHSMARSCHALL

One important factor in the battle was the calibre of its senior players. Sir Hugh Dowding had a lifetime career in both the Army and the RAF, at every level of responsibility. He was highly qualified and highly respected by his staff. Hermann Göring, on the other hand, the head of the Luftwaffe, although a First World War squadron leader and fighter ace with twenty-two confirmed kills to his name, had carved out a political career with the Nazi Party between the wars. He had no real relevant experience and was detested by many of the officers under his command, some of whom regarded him as a figure of ridicule and repulsion. Even in Britain, his elaborate self-styled uniforms made him the butt of many jokes and cartoons.

By 1940 Göring had risen to become deputy chancellor of the Reich, head of the Air Ministry, and commander-in-chief of the Luftwaffe. In July 1940, following the success of the continental Blitzkrieg, he was elevated to the unique rank of Reichsmarschall, which translates as 'Empire Marshal'.

MAKE-UP OF THE LUFTWAFFE

The Luftwaffe was divided into air fleets known as Luftflottes, and for the campaign against Britain three such bodies were deployed: Luftflotte 2, commanded by Field-Marshal Albert Kesselring; Luftflotte 3, under Field-Marshal

Map showing how the Luftwaffe had established a battle line against Britain in July 1940 that stretched from Stavanger in Norway to Cherbourg in France.

Hugo von Sperrle; and Luftflotte 5, under General Hans-Jurgen Stumpff. Each Luftflotte would have a bomber arm known as the *kampfgeschwader*, and a fighter arm to provide support for the bombers, known as the *jagdgeschwader*.

As a general rule, each of these air fleets was further sub-divided into air corps known as *fliegerkorps*, which were themselves broken into formations called *geschwaders*. There were also sub-units or divisions, known as *fliegerdivisions*. A *geschwader* was normally made up of three operational wings known as *gruppen*, along with a headquarters flight and a reserve or training *gruppe*. Each *gruppe* comprised of three squadrons or staffels of nine aircraft each. For combat purposes the Fighter Command pilots normally flew in sections of three aircraft, whereas the Germans flew in *schwarms* of four aircraft, with the smallest combat formation being a *rotte*, consisting of two aircraft.

Luftflotte 2 had its headquarters in Brussels, with corps' headquarters at Beauvais, Ghent and Haarlem. Luftflotte 3 was headquartered at Saint-Cloud, near Paris, with corps based at Villacoublay, Dinard and Deauville. These two formations would provide the attack force against southern England and the industrial Midlands. Luftflotte 5 was based in Denmark and Norway for assaults on Scotland and the north of England. What this effectively meant was that by July 1940, the Luftwaffe had established a battle line against Britain that stretched from Stavanger in Norway to Cherbourg in France.

MESSERSCHMITT BF 109E

If the Spitfire was the icon of British air fighting at the time, in Germany the Messerschmitt Bf 109E was held in similar esteem; during the daily battles of

A Messerschmitt Bf 109E in Battle of Britain livery at the Farnborough Air Show in 2010. (Copyright Steve Daniels and licensed for reuse under the Creative Commons Licence)

1940 it proved itself to be the biggest threat to the survival of Fighter Command. Spitfires and Hurricanes could easily and confidently deal with all of the German bombers, but in the Messerschmitt Bf 109E they found a worthy and often deadly opponent.

The Me 109 was designed by Willi Messerschmitt and manufactured by Messerschmitt A. G. of Augsburg. It was powered by a Daimler-Benz DB 601A engine and had a maximum speed of 354 mph. Only the Spitfire could match its speed. It was armed with two 20mm cannon in the wings and two 7.9mm machine guns, firing between the blades of the propeller. The prototype first flew in September 1935, ironically powered by a Rolls-Royce Kestrel engine. Its main task during the Battle of Britain was to fly with the bombers to provide them with protection.

The Me 109 might have been faster than the Hurricane, but against the Spitfire it found its equal. However, it did have some advantages over the British fighter. The 109's Daimler-Benz engine was fitted with a fuel injection system, whereas the Merlin engine of the Spitfire had a carburettor petrol feed. In a dogfight, when subjected to violent manoeuvres, the Merlin might become starved of fuel, making the engine momentarily stall, while in a similar situation the 109's engine continued to perform efficiently. The 109 also performed better at higher altitudes, although in later versions of both the Spitfire and the Hurricane this particular deficiency was rectified with the development of the variable-pitch propeller. The other advantage that the 109 had over its rivals was its 20mm cannons, which were far superior to the Browning machine guns of the British.

MESSERSCHMITT BF 110

The Messerschmitt Bf 110 was a two-seater fighter aircraft, intended to be a long-range escort fighter for Göring's bombers. The idea was to use it ahead of the bomber formations to sweep the enemy out of the sky. However, this tactic soon failed against Fighter Command and the Bf 110 had to resign itself to providing close escort for the bombers instead.

It was manufactured by Messerschmitt A. G. and first flown in 1936. It was powered by two Daimler-Benz DB 601A engines and had a top speed of 249 mph. It was armed with four 7.9mm MG17 machine guns and two 20mm MGFF cannon firing forward, with one MG15 machine gun for rear defence. The standard range of the Bf 110 was 680 miles, but it could be fitted with drop fuel tanks that enabled it to accompany bombers on longer missions over Britain,

This detail from a sign at the Battle of Britain public house in Northfleet, Gravesend, shows a Messerschmitt Bf 110 as it tumbles to earth with one engine on fire. (Copyright Henry Buckton)

whereas the Me 109 was almost totally restricted to the south and south-east.

Göring put a lot of faith in the Messerschmitt Bf 110, calling it the 'Zerstörer' which meant the 'Destroyer'. However, Lord Beaverbrook's assessment proved to be spot on; it was not as manoeuvrable as the Hurricane, nor as fast as the Spitfire, and on occasion had to be escorted itself by 109s, which rather defeated the object.

THE ENEMY BOMBER FORCE

As for the German bombers, the Junkers Ju 88 was made by Junkers Flugzeug-und Motorenwerke AG of Dessau. First flown in 1936 it had two Junkers Jumo engines. It had a maximum speed of 286 mph and carried a crew of four as well as a two-ton bomb load. There were two versions used in the battle, the A-1 and the A-5. To protect itself from enemy fighter attack it carried three machine guns in the dorsal, ventral and nose positions, although another gun was later added to the dorsal position. It was very poorly armoured and an easy prey to any of the British fighters.

The Junkers Ju 87, known as the 'Stuka', shortened from Sturzkampfflugzeug which meant dive-attack aircraft, was also manufactured by Junkers Flugzeug-und Motorenwerke AG. It was used in the dive-bombing and ground attack roles in which it was lethal to its enemy if left unchallenged. It was fitted with a siren which gave out an ear-piercing scream as it dropped out of the sky in a near vertical dive, a sound that terrified anyone below. However for all of this it was extremely vulnerable to both British fighters and anti-aircraft guns. It was powered by a Junkers Jumo 211DA engine, but only had a maximum speed of 232 mph, which left it floundering against a Hurricane or Spitfire. It fared so badly over England in the summer of 1940 that it had to be withdrawn from daylight operations.

The Heinkel He 111 was manufactured by Ernst Heinkel Flugzeugwerke GmbH of Marienehe and Oranienburg. It was probably the most famous and recognisable of all the German long-range bombers. It was powered by either two Daimler-Benz DB 601A engines or two Junkers Jumo 211 engines. Its maiden flight was in 1935 and it catered for a crew of between five and six. It had a maximum speed of 255 mph and a range of 760 miles when fully laden with bombs. It had the capacity to carry up to two tons of bombs, and when fitted with external bomb racks this was increased to two and a half tons. Many variants of the Heinkel He 111 were used during the Battle.

The Dornier Do 17 was used as both a long-range bomber and a reconnaissance aircraft. It was manufactured by Dornier-Werke GmbH of Neuaubing and Friedrichshafen. Its maiden flight was in 1937 and because of its slim, sleek appearance, it became known as 'the flying pencil'. There were many variants of this aircraft so the following are the average statistics based on the Dornier Do 17Z-2. It was powered by two Bramo 323P radial engines and had a maximum speed of 265 mph when carrying a ton of bombs. With a full bomb-load it had a range of around 750 miles. The Dornier Do 215 was virtually the same aircraft, except it was powered by two Daimler-Benz DB 601A engines.

The Focke-Wulf 200 was only used in very small numbers during the battle. It was manufactured by Focke-Wulf Flugzeugbau GmbH of Cottbus. It was powered by four BMW 132H-I radial engines and had a maximum speed of 250 mph. Known as the 'Condor', it was developed as a long-range civil transport aircraft, but it was also used on armed reconnaissance missions. It was armed with three machine guns and one 20mm cannon. When used as a bomber it could carry one ton of bombs and had a range of 2,430 miles. In the Battle of Britain it was only used for a short period in August during night raids on Liverpool.

Heinkel He 111 long-range bomber, which was used widely throughout the battle. (Copyright Clemens Vasters and licensed for reuse under the Creative Commons Licence)

3

PHASE ONE – THE BATTLE FOR THE ENGLISH CHANNEL

On 10 July 1940, the size and preparedness of the German Air Force poised for the attack on the French side of the English Channel was formidable, to say the least, and would not be easy for Air Chief Marshal Dowding and Fighter Command to combat. But all over Britain men were ready to do their duty and play their part in one of the most important events in modern history.

10 JULY – THE BATTLE COMMENCES

Since the fall of France on 22 June, the Germans had mounted numerous sorties over or towards Britain, including one on the morning of 10 July, when at approximately 1100 hours a convoy of ships was attacked off North Foreland by a solitary Dornier Do 17Z, escorted by ten Messerschmitt Bf 109Es. However, the afternoon plots building up on the No. 11 Group operations room table at RAF Uxbridge seemed to be on a much larger scale than usual.

On the afternoon of 10 July, RDF stations in the Dover area reported that across the English Channel aircraft were beginning to mass behind the Pas de Calais. Something was undoubtedly brewing and it soon became evident that the Germans were mustering to attack a convoy of ships that was heading west through the Channel.

In response, Air Vice-Marshal Keith Park at RAF Uxbridge vectored a flight of six patrolling Hurricanes of No. 32 Squadron to the area, which had been flying that day from the sector airfield at Biggin Hill. He also scrambled a further flight of six Hurricanes of No. 56 Squadron, who were at readiness at their forward base at RAF Manston near Ramsgate. By the time these fighters arrived on the scene the convoy was already being attacked by around seventy enemy aircraft.

The Germans had formed up in three aerial layers. The bottom layer was made up of the bombers, in this instance around twenty Dornier Do 17Zs. Above the bombers was a group of some thirty Messerschmitt Bf 110s that were

Battle for the Channel: Ju 88As attack a convoy of ships as Spitfires go in for the kill. (Copyright Joe Crowfoot)

there to provide them with close support, and at the very top were around twenty Messerschmitt Bf 109Es acting as top guard. This would prove to be the standard Luftwaffe formation for much of the battle. The idea of this formation was that once the bombers were engaged by the enemy, the Bf 110s would form a defensive circle around them to hold the attackers at bay, while the Bf 109s, with their advantage of height and speed, would swoop down for the kill.

In an act of what can only be described as heroism of the highest order in the face of such overwhelming odds and indicative of the flyers of Fighter Command in the coming weeks, the twelve Hurricane pilots waded in. Some of them attacked the bombers while others took on the Bf 110s. In response to this, the Bf 109s immediately dived to engage them.

On paper, the Hurricane pilots should have been annihilated but instead all survived and returned to their bases, although one No. 56 Squadron aircraft crash-landed on arrival back at Manston, while a No. 32 Squadron Hurricane crash-landed at Lympne and another at Hawkinge. Soon the fighters of several

Four Me 109s cross the English Channel during the summer of 1940.

other squadrons had joined the fray and the attack was beaten off, but only after one of the ships in the convoy had been sunk.

Further raids continued throughout the day on targets ranging from the Firth of Tay to Beachy Head, which included attacks on shipping and one or two aerodromes. At the close of play the RAF had flown 641 individual sorties and had lost six aircraft. The Luftwaffe had lost eight fighters and four bombers: the Battle of Britain had officially begun.

Surprisingly, the first British pilot to be killed during the Battle of Britain did not take part in the above-mentioned action. Sergeant Pilot Ian Charles Cooper Clenshaw of No. 253 Squadron died at 0959 hours on 10 July, flying Hurricane No. P3359 while on a dawn patrol in poor visibility. His aircraft went out of control and crashed in the Humber Estuary.

Dover patrol: Spitfires are pictured patrolling along the white cliffs. (Copyright Joe Crowfoot)

THE LUFTWAFFE PLAN (ADLERANGRIFF)

Over the next few days and throughout the opening part of the battle, convoys and naval facilities remained the Luftwaffe's priority. The Germans would also drop mines into the English Channel and around the approaches to ports. The British were also laying mines, so the whole process of navigation became doubly precarious.

In the coming days the Luftwaffe planned to make a great attack designed at defeating Fighter Command both in the air and on the ground, as a prelude to invasion. This plan was code-named Adlerangriff, or 'Eagle Attack', and would be launched on Adlertag, 'Eagle Day'. The date of Adlertag was yet to be announced while, in the meantime, the Luftwaffe kept up its attacks in the Channel. On 11 July, for instance, another convoy of ships was attacked off the Dorset coast and naval installations around Portland and Portsmouth were also hit. On 12 July convoys were targeted off Orford Ness in Suffolk and North Foreland in

Kent, while on the 13 July two convoys were attacked off Harwich and on the 14 July another was mauled near Dover. All of these attacks indicated that Göring's opening mandate for the battle was to win control of the English Channel and the Straits of Dover. On 14 July Churchill broadcast the following to the nation:

> The RAF have shot down more than five to one of the German aircraft which have tried to molest our convoys in the Channel or ventured to cross the British coast... should the invader come, there will be no placid lying down of the people in submission before him. We shall defend every village, every town and every city.

Luftwaffe aircrews receive their final briefing before a mission over Britain, here being given directional instructions.

Convoys Come Under Attack

It was on 11 July that Douglas Bader of No. 242 Squadron, one of the great characters to emerge from the struggle, made his first kill of the battle, a Dornier Do 17. Also during this period it became clear that the Germans were using Red Cross planes on supposed air-sea rescue missions to reconnoitre the convoys, so the government took the unusual step of announcing that they were no longer immune from attack.

Poor weather conditions over the Channel and southern England between 15–18 July brought a reduction in aerial activity, although during breaks in the rain or fog, ships and harbours were still harassed when possible. Other targets included the Westland aircraft factory in Yeovil and RAF St Athan.

Because of these early attacks directed against convoys, Air Chief Marshal Dowding became increasingly alarmed at the number of routine patrols his aircraft were committed to fly in order to protect the ships. The early warning system based around the employment of RDF and the Observer Corps had been devised to maximise the potential of Fighter Command and minimise wasted patrol hours and fuel. With the same foresight that had pitted him against Churchill when he was set on a course of sending vital squadrons to France, Dowding made it clear to the Air Ministry and the Admiralty that compliance with their demand to give fighter cover to all convoys would leave British airspace dangerously exposed. It would effectively play into Göring's hands and could lead to the defeat of Fighter Command and ultimately Britain itself. He insisted that when the real battle began the defence of Britain itself would take precedence, even if it meant convoys went unprotected. Although Dowding was making few friends in high places, he was making critical decisions that could save the nation.

The job of advising Hitler about when would be a good time to mount the invasion of England was given to Major Josef Schmid, who was the head of his intelligence service. Based on a report submitted to him by Schmid, Hitler issued Directive No. 16 on 16 July. This Directive demanded that preparations for the invasion of England, code-named Operation Sealion (*Seelöwe*) would begin at once. Schmid's review of the apparent strength and capabilities of both the RAF and the Luftwaffe favoured the success of the latter, as long as large-scale operations began early enough to exploit the relatively favourable weather conditions that were predicted for much of that summer. Hitler's directive included the words,

The tail fin of a Junkers
Ju 87 Stuka with marks
showing missions flown
over Norway and Britain,
as well as one ship sunk.

Since England, in spite of her hopeless military situation, shows no sign of being
ready to come to terms, I have decided to prepare a landing operation. But first
the English air force must be so disabled in spirit and in fact that it cannot
deliver any significant attack on the German crossing.

The final plans that were drawn up for Operation Sealion were a compromise
between what the Army wanted, and what the Navy agreed was possible. On 21
July, as raids continued on convoys in the Channel, Hitler summoned his service
chiefs to a meeting in order to discuss the plans.

General Halder, chief of the Army general staff, insisted that, in order to
guarantee the success of the operation, forty divisions would be needed. This
monumental task would involve the Navy landing an initial 250,000 troops along
a 100-mile stretch of England's south coast. However, in view of the unrealistic

timescale, Navy chiefs would only accept responsibility for transporting ten divisions. Grand-Admiral Raeder proposed landing 160,000 troops on a much narrower, forty-mile front, between Eastbourne and Dover. This brought the Army and Navy into deeper conflict, but also meant that, with so few troops in the first wave, the success of them being able to secure a beachhead was seriously in doubt.

Göring insisted that with five days of fine weather he would be able to completely subdue Fighter Command and gain air supremacy. This encouraged Hitler into maintaining his hope that Britain would ultimately capitulate once the invasion had begun, in which instance, ten divisions would be ample for occupation purposes. All parties agreed that the key to success was in the hands of the Luftwaffe. In fact, Hitler was so confident of success that discussions were entered into about how to administrate the country once Churchill had surrendered.

A model Spitfire stands over a building at the Tangmere Military Aviation Museum, which is situated on part of the Battle of Britain airfield and contains evocative displays from the time. (Copyright Henry Buckton)

A Boulton Paul Defiant of No. 264 Squadron. The Defiant showed its vulnerability on Friday 19 July when six out of a flying compliment of nine aircraft of No. 141 Squadron were shot down off Dover. (Copyright Joe Crowfoot)

Eventually it was agreed that the Kriegsmarine would indeed transport 160,000 initial troops. They would be ferried in barges, requisitioned fishing boats and tugs, all of which would be guided by naval craft through a narrow corridor. Both sides of this corridor would be mined and guarded by U-boats. Embarkation points for the invasion would stretch from Le Havre in the south, to Rotterdam in the north. Overall command of the operation was given to Gerd von Rundstedt, who had been promoted to Field Marshal on 19 July. But all of this would take time to organise and in the meantime the battles over the Channel continued.

FIGHTER COMMAND SUFFERS A BLOW

After the opening nine days of battle, the score, in terms of aircraft lost, was definitely to the advantage of Fighter Command, who had lost twenty-eight compared to the Luftwaffe's sixty-one. However, the first major setback for Dowding occurred on Friday 19 July, when six Boulton Paul Defiants of No.

Ginger Lacey, top-scoring British Hurricane pilot of the battle, is seen on the left of this picture with fellow 501 Squadron pilots Mac Mackenzie, Tony Whitehouse, Bob Dafforn and Vic Ekins. (Courtesy of Severnside Aviation Society)

141 Squadron, out of a flying compliment of nine, were shot down off Dover. This tragedy only helped to highlight the vulnerability of using these aircraft in daylight fighter operations against Me 109s.

In total, the RAF lost eleven aircraft on the day against only two for the enemy. For the British this was a crippling blow for both equipment and the morale of personnel. Also on 19 July, Hitler made another appeal to the British asking their leaders to see 'common sense' and bring an end to the war. He added that if the war did continue it could only end in the annihilation of either Britain or Germany.

A CHANGE OF STRATEGY

Thanks to the changeable weather over the next couple of days, Kesselring and von Sperrle were unable to mount any significant operations and did little more than harass shipping. But on 22 July the weather broke and Kesselring took the opportunity to mount simultaneous attacks on convoys in the Straits of Dover

BRITISH FIGHTER ACES

The Battle of Britain, fought between the brave young airmen of Fighter Command and the Luftwaffe, would see the names of several of these elevated into household names. Britain in particular needed heroes to boost the country's morale and, although every one of 'the Few' is rightly considered a hero, several fighter aces stood out for their prowess.

On 20 July the RAF shot down nine German aircraft for the loss of three of their own. One of the enemy aircraft, which was a Messerschmitt Bf 109E, was the first kill during the battle of No. 501 Squadron's Sergeant James Harry 'Ginger' Lacey, who, having already claimed five victories in France, went on to be the RAF's top-scoring Hurricane pilot in the Battle of Britain with fifteen and a half confirmed kills. On this particular occasion, No. 501 Squadron had been scrambled from Middle Wallop and vectored to a point between Jersey and Portland Bill, where a convoy was under attack from Ju 87s escorted by Me 109s.

Pilot Officer Eric Lock of No 41 Squadron was destined to become the top scoring British Spitfire pilot of the battle, with sixteen and a half kills, the first of which was a Me 110 on 15 August.

and Thames Estuary. During the latter, Major Adolf Galland, one of Germany's top-scoring pilots, led the Me 109s of JG 26 into action over Britain for the first time to escort the bombers. However, Keith Park acted with calm restraint, ever mindful of keeping enough aircraft in reserve to counter any further threats. This somewhat frustrated the Germans, who were unable to deliver the blow to Fighter Command that they had wished. The British fighters that did enter combat fought with such ferocity that they compelled Galland to report that the RAF were proving to be 'a most formidable opponent'.

On 25 July a convoy of twenty-one merchant ships escorted by two armed trawlers and six Hurricanes left Southend. Having detected the convoy, Adolf Galland's fighters escorted around sixty Ju 87s in for the kill. They were successful in sinking five of the merchantmen and severely damaging another six. The commander of naval forces in Dover, Vice-Admiral Sir Bertram Ramsay, sent out two destroyers to deal with an E-boat flotilla that had joined the fight. Having

successfully seen these off the two destroyers were themselves dive-bombed and damaged.

The destruction of this convoy was a bitter pill for the British to swallow and forced the Admiralty into rethinking its strategy of sending merchant traffic through the Straits of Dover in daylight. On the positive side, the air fighting still favoured Fighter Command, who dispatched sixteen of the enemy for the loss of seven.

While the Admiralty took stock of the situation and contemplated their options, convoys virtually ceased. One or two small groups did make passage by laboriously sailing at night and harbouring by day in ports along the south coast. This was not very helpful to the Luftwaffe's master plan of defeating the RAF by drawing them into combat over the sea. So with very few sea-going ships to target, Kesselring and von Sperrle turned their attentions to attacking ports instead. Dover was hit on several occasions, while other targets extended from Plymouth to Belfast. But at this time numerous attacks were also made against industrial targets throughout Britain, which included many on aircraft factories. If they could stop the production of new aircraft and prevent any from reaching the RAF, Fighter Command could be crippled. Of course, with no convoys to

Vice-Admiral Sir Bertram Ramsay, commander of naval forces in Dover, conducted naval operations in the Straits of Dover during the Battle of Britain from within Dover Castle, where this statue now overlooks the straits towards France. (Copyright Karen Roe and licensed for reuse under the Creative Commons Licence)

protect, Dowding's group commanders didn't have to waste aircraft on standing patrols and could more effectively deal with these other incursions.

BRITAIN LOSES CONTROL OF THE STRAITS OF DOVER

There is no doubt that if an invasion was to be attempted, the momentum was beginning to grow. Although few merchant ships now plied the Straits, Ramsay certainly guarded the waters between Dover and Calais with destroyers, this being the most likely crossing point for the Nazis. However, on 27 July Luftflotte 2 managed to sink two of these, while on the 29 July Luftflotte 3 sank a third. The Admiralty had no option but to acknowledge that they no longer had control of the Straits during daylight hours. The following day Hitler ordered Göring to

The Gallant Few by Joe Crowfoot. Spitfires attack a formation of enemy bombers as they break apart. (Copyright Joe Crowfoot)

be ready to unleash his main assault at twelve hours' notice, the purpose of which would be the total subjugation of Fighter Command as a pre-cursor to invasion.

The planning for the invasion, Hitler informed the chiefs of staff on Wednesday 31 July, must be completed by the end of August and the invasion itself executed by 15 September. In Directive No. 17, issued on 1 August, he outlined how the Luftwaffe would achieve the final defeat of the RAF. First by the destruction of its aircraft, both in the air and on the ground, then their ground support organisation and fuel supplies. Next would come the total disruption of aircraft production lines, as well as factories manufacturing anti-aircraft weapons. In response, Göring issued orders for Adlertag, on which Luftflottes 2 and 3 would begin the final process, expected to take seventy-two hours of fine continuous weather to achieve. Initially, 10 August was penciled in as the starting date.

CONVOY PEEWIT

The next drama of any note began to unfold on the evening of Wednesday 7 August, when the first ships to assemble in the Thames Estuary since the

Admiralty had rethought convoy protection set sail. The plan was for the twenty merchant ships and their nine naval escorts to leave the Medway and pass through the Straits of Dover under the cover of darkness. Previously such convoys were normally protected by armed trawlers, but this one, code-named 'Peewit' by the RAF, was accompanied by two destroyers fitted with improved anti-aircraft armaments. Barrage balloons would also guard the ships, from specially-modified boats designed to deter dive-bombers. At first light the ships would be further escorted by fighter aircraft as they steamed westward along the south coast towards Swanage.

Although the Germans had paid little attention to the British RDF chain up until this point, they had in fact been developing their own form of radar for shipping and, unfortunately for 'Peewit', a new Freya radar site had been set up on the coast near Calais, which detected the convoy as it passed. E-Boats were immediately sent and sank three of the merchantmen. Then, at around 0900, Luftflotte 3 went in to finish the rest off near Brighton.

In the second phase of the battle the Luftwaffe would attack Fighter Command airfields. Here we see the preserved Battle of Britain operations room at RAF Duxford in Cambridgeshire. (Copyright Jon's Pics and licensed for reuse under the Creative Commons Licence)

Hugo von Sperrle saw this as an ideal opportunity to both test the accuracy of his Stuka dive-bombers and engage Fighter Command with his Me 109s. The latter he did, but to his consternation the Hurricanes and Spitfires sent against him repelled successive attacks. However, just after midday the defenders were overwhelmed by German reinforcements and another four merchantmen were sunk. Only a quarter of the convoy finally reached its destination, but at the end of the day the Luftwaffe had lost thirty-one aircraft to the RAF's nineteen.

The attack on 'Peewit' was so massive and sustained that to the Air Ministry it seemed as though the stakes had been raised. The order of the day promulgated: 'The Battle of Britain is about to begin. Members of the Royal Air Force, the fate of generations lie in your hands.'

B Flight of No. 501 Squadron outside the dispersal tent at Hawkinge in August 1940. (Courtesy of Severnside Aviation Society)

4

PHASE TWO – FIGHTER COMMAND COMES UNDER ATTACK

The second phase of the battle began on 13 August 1940, when the Germans discontinued their attacks on convoys of ships passing through the English Channel as a means of attracting the aircraft of Britain's defence force into engagements over the sea and, instead, turned their full force against Fighter Command itself as a prelude to invasion. Their plan was to attack airfields and make them inoperable, while at the same time destroying Dowding's aircraft both in the air and on the ground. If they could knock out all of the airfields so that they could not be used by aircraft for landing or taking off, Fighter Command would be unable to attack the German invasion fleet as it crossed the Channel. The assault on Fighter Command would begin on Adlertag, or Eagle Day. Adlertag had already been postponed on a number of occasions, but on the 13 August Hitler was determined that it should proceed.

PREPARING FOR EAGLE DAY

Eagle Day was initially penned in for 10 August, but poor weather, with a cocktail of cloud, wind, rain and thunderstorms, meant that it had to be postponed until 0530 on Tuesday 13 August.

On 11 and 12 August, Göring began the process of softening up specified targets in preparation for the great day. These included the Dover balloon barrage, Portland naval base, Portsmouth docks and Hastings. The Luftwaffe also began to target RDF stations such as those at Ventnor on the Isle of Wight, Dunkirk in Kent, and Dover itself, where the aerial masts on the white cliffs were damaged. Ventnor was actually put out of action, although the Germans were probably not aware of it. There were also heavy attacks on several airfields, notably Manston, Hawkinge and Lympne.

During the morning of Monday 12 August, among the Luftwaffe's targets were two small convoys, 'Agent' and 'Arena', that were passing North Foreland, so attacks on shipping would still feature in the overall plan.

Rare wartime colour photograph of a Messerschmitt Bf 109E in flight. (Copyright Paul Chryst)

ADLERTAG (EAGLE DAY) – 13 AUGUST

Unfortunately for the Germans, on the morning of Eagle Day much of south-east England was once again covered in a blanket of fog. At the very last moment Göring had little alternative but to postpone the attack until later that day. However, the message did not reach, or was not understood by, the leaders of one or two formations, including that of KG2 led by Oberst Johannes Fink. He rendezvoused as arranged at 0530 and even though he found himself without fighter escorts he still set course for his objectives, the RAF aerodrome at Eastchurch in the Isle of Sheppey and the naval facility at Sheerness. After being detected by RDF, No. 74 Spitfire Squadron was scrambled to intercept.

Part of the German force did eventually locate Eastchurch through a break in the fog and their Do 17s cratered the airfield with their bombs. They also damaged station buildings and destroyed five Blenheims on the ground. The Hurricanes of No. 111 and No. 151 Squadrons had soon joined in, and as the raiders turned for home four were shot down and another four badly damaged. The irony of this opening attack perhaps exemplifies not so much the lack of intelligence that the Germans had gathered, but their misunderstanding of it. Eastchurch was in fact a Coastal Command station, although the Luftwaffe might have argued that it could have been used to accommodate Fighter Command as an emergency measure, as it unquestionably was from time to time.

Later that morning, over twenty Me 110s crossed the coast near Portland. This was unusual because the 110s were normally employed as close escort fighters for the bombers, but in this instance there were no bombers in sight. They were in fact a decoy designed to draw Fighter Command away from a genuine raid that was to follow. It was successful in provoking combat, during which two Spitfires and five of the Me 110s were shot down. However, it was unsuccessful in its main purpose because the subsequent bombers arrived late, and by the time the real raid manifested the decoy action had been over for some time and the British had already refuelled and rearmed. To make matters worse, when the Stukas did arrive, persisting cloud cover meant they were unable to dive-bomb their targets, so they returned home with their loads intact.

But the story of Göring's long-promised Adlertag was not one of total blundering on the part of the Germans. Several targets were hit, and of course

Typical RAF Control Tower, in this instance at Manston in Kent, which was one of the most targeted airfields in the country during the Battle of Britain. (Copyright Calfileroo1 and licensed for reuse under the Creative Commons Licence)

this was only the start of a sustained campaign to wear down and destroy Fighter Command. For instance, the airfields at Detling, Middle Wallop and Andover all took punishment of various degrees. Southampton docks were badly damaged and Canterbury was bombed when a raid on a nearby airfield failed to find its target and the perpetrators jettisoned their cargo. Raids on the airfields at Farnborough and Odiham were successfully driven off and during the night there were widespread attacks on Scotland, the West Country, Norwich and the Midlands, where the Morris works at Castle Bromwich were hit. At the close of play the Luftwaffe had lost thirty-four aircraft and the RAF thirteen.

THE DAY AFTER

At the end of Adlertag, much to Hitler's exasperation, Fighter Command still had control of British airspace. Having said that, Eagle Day was only intended to be the start of the five days of constant bombardment that Göring had boasted would be all he needed to finish Fighter Command off. So events over the next few days would follow a similar pattern. There would be several raids, involving hundreds of bombers supported by Me 110s, while gaggles of Me 109s were given free range to roam the sky hoping to secure an all-out fighter battle. To fulfill his vow, Fighter Command would be finished by the 17 August, although the one thing that Göring couldn't predict was the British weather.

On Wednesday 14 August, once again the weather played its role in foiling the Luftwaffe's plans. Because of cloud, the day's intended programme was postponed until the following day, but Kesselring and von Sperrle were still able to launch numerous raids against priority targets, including aircraft factories, RDF sites and the airfields at Manston, Hawkinge, Colerne, Sealand, Middle Wallop, and Lympne. Barrage balloons were shot down over Dover and Folkestone, and railway lines were attacked in several places including Southampton. Some of these attacks were merely nuisance raids carried out by solitary bombers and, at the airfields, damaged runways were quickly repaired.

At this time many in Britain would listen to the daily propaganda broadcasts made from Berlin by the traitor William Joyce, better known as 'Lord Haw-Haw'. In these messages he reported that crippling losses had been suffered by the RAF. In a bid to reassure people that Fighter Command was still in control, aircraft landing and sometimes taking off from Manston were instructed to fly low over Ramsgate or Dover. And also, to show that both the RAF and the Royal Navy had not lost control of the Channel, lightly laden ships began to use it again. As well as boosting civilian morale, this show of defiance and strength was aimed at the world's media, who had been gathering in the south-east corner of England ready to report on the defeat of Britain and the success of the anticipated invasion.

BLACK THURSDAY – 15 AUGUST

Thursday August 15 would prove to be one of the most influential days on the outcome of the entire battle. It produced the hardest fighting of the period and the Luftwaffe's biggest single daily loss of aircraft. At the end of play, seventy-five raiders lay burning in the British countryside or floating in the sea. To the Germans it became known as 'Black Thursday'.

For the first time during the battle, all three German air fleets would attack Britain at the same time. A mass of machines would take off from bases along the entire Nazi front. This would include the first raid comprising more than 100 aircraft on the north of England.

Opposing fighters: this photograph taken at RIAT in 2010 shows the difference in size and shape between the Spitfire and the Me 109. (Copyright Airwolfhound and licensed for reuse under the Creative Commons Licence)

General Stumpff's armada from Luftflotte 5 consisted of approximately sixty-five Heinkel 111s, fifty Junkers 88s, and thirty-five Messerschmitt 110s. He divided his force in two. The Heinkels escorted by the 110s headed for airfields in the Newcastle-upon-Tyne area, while the faster Ju 88s flew unescorted to bomb airfields in Yorkshire.

RDF detected the Heinkels and their escorts early, and No. 72 Spitfire Squadron was scrambled from Acklington, meeting them well out at sea. After a moment of overwhelmed hesitation the eleven Spitfires, led by Flight-Lieutenant Edward Graham, went into a diving attack on their adversaries, numbering over a hundred.

During the melee some of the Germans dropped almost to sea level and headed for home. Those that remained split into two sections, one of which attempted to reach the No. 13 Group sector station at Usworth, while the other tried to attack the aerodromes at Linton-upon-Ouse and Dishforth. Neither raid was successful.

While all of this was going on the Ju 88s were heading towards the airfield at Great Driffield. Two squadrons were scrambled from Church Fenton, but a few of the Junkers did manage to slip through the net and attack the aerodrome.

Detail from a stained glass window at St George's Chapel of Remembrance at RAF Biggin Hill. Here we see WAAFs at the map table plotting a raid as it happens. Quite possibly the German air chiefs underestimated the sophistication of Fighter Command's warning system. (Copyright Loco Steve and licensed for reuse under the Creative Commons Licence)

However, Luftflotte 5 was so badly depleted during these actions that it never again attempted another large-scale daylight raid on the north of Britain. The fact was that its bombers were too vulnerable without proper fighter protection.

In the southern half of Britain, Kesselring and von Sperrle were decidedly more successful, with Manston, Hawkinge and Croydon among the airfields badly hit. During the night the onslaught continued with bombing runs on numerous industrial and civilian centres. By the end of Black Thursday the Luftwaffe had flown 1,786 individual sorties, the most it would fly in any single day. Fighter Command had survived its toughest day of the battle so far.

GERMANY'S POOR INTELLIGENCE OVERESTIMATES RAF LOSSES

On Friday 16 August, Göring set out to maintain the scale of the previous day's attacks; there was no easing now if his plan was to succeed. Although he had

FOR CONSPICUOUS GALLANTRY

It was during the attack on Gosport on 16 August that the actions of Flight-Lieutenant James Nicholson of No. 249 Squadron led to the award of Fighter Command's only Victoria Cross of the battle. The squadron was based at Boscombe Down and equipped with Hurricanes. On the day in question they were vectored towards the coast. Red section consisted of Squadron Leader Eric King, Flight Lieutenant James Nicholson and Pilot Officer Martyn King. Suddenly they were bounced by enemy fighters and all three aircraft were damaged. Squadron Leader Eric King managed to nurse his Hurricane back to Boscombe but Pilot Officer Martyn King was forced to bail out of his aircraft. Unfortunately, his parachute collapsed and he plunged to his death.

Nicholson's aircraft had been engulfed by flames after the fuel tank had ignited. But despite suffering terrible burns and being wounded by the cannon fire, he remained in his burning cockpit and only bailed out once he had pursed and shot down a Messerschmitt Bf 110. To add pain to his injuries, as he finally descended in his parachute he was shot in the buttocks by a member of the Local Defence Volunteers. Thankfully he survived all of these injuries and for his valour that day, he was given the nation's highest award.

sustained massive losses in aircraft, his intelligence gatherers insisted that the RAF had fared even worse. Sources informed him that even with replacements arriving from the factories, Dowding was down to 430 aircraft, of which only 300 were operational. If these figures were to be believed, Göring had every reason to assume that his all-out assault on Fighter Command was beginning to work; surely after a few more days like these, Dowding would be on his knees? The reality was actually very different, as Fighter Command still had 750 Hurricanes and Spitfires, 102 Defiants, Gladiators and Blenheims and a reserve compliment of 235 Hurricanes and Spitfires. On paper, the fighter forces of both sides were by now quite evenly balanced.

One thing to the Luftwaffe's advantage was that they could still concentrate all of their fighters on the south-east if necessary, whereas Dowding's were distributed throughout Britain to tackle the bomber threat wherever it manifested. Also, at any one time several RAF squadrons were away from the front line, resting and refitting. Therefore, in the event of an all-out fighter battle in the south-east, the Luftwaffe's short-range fighters could still outnumber Park's Spitfires and Hurricanes by at least two to one. But what Dowding certainly did not have enough of were trained pilots. He had an establishment for 1,558 pilots but was now down to only 1,379. Fully trained replacements were slow in filtering through.

On 16 August airfields were again the principal targets of the day's activity, but if Göring's plan was to smash Fighter Command, once again, his intelligence source seems questionable. Of the selected targets, only Tangmere, Westhampnett, Manston and West Malling were fighter stations. The latter was hit particularly badly and was unusable for the next four days. Other airfields hit included Coastal Command or naval stations such as Lee-on-Solent and Gosport. During these attacks the Luftwaffe destroyed several aircraft on the ground, but only three of these were fighters.

Keeping up the Pressure

During the night of 16 August bombs were dropped on Chester, Newport, Bristol, Swansea, Portland, Tavistock and Worcester. Throughout the day the Luftwaffe flew some 1,700 sorties; although it was relatively successful and their losses were not as great as on the previous day, they still lost forty-five aircraft.

The RDF station at Ventnor on the Isle of Wight, which had already been damaged a few days previously, was bombed again on the 16 August and this time put out of action until 23 August. This left a dangerous gap in the radar chain, which compromised the system's effectiveness. However, for some reason, Göring was reluctant to sanction attacks on RDF sites. Perhaps he still did not appreciate how important they were, or perhaps he just wished to destroy airfields and aircraft as quickly as possible and RDF sites were a distraction from this main purpose. So, with a few isolated exceptions, the Luftwaffe failed to follow up its attacks on RDF sites, which proved to be a costly tactical error.

Signs of Discontent Within the Luftwaffe

After two days of heavy and sustained attacks the Luftwaffe surprised the British by mounting no major attacks on Saturday 17 August, despite it being a fine summer's day. Göring had promised a five day continuous onslaught against Fighter Command, but with his enemy reeling, for some unaccountable reason he took a day's respite. It is quite probable that he was sympathetic to the fact that his pilots were becoming frustrated and weary by the lack of evident progress.

Heat of the Battle by Joe Crowfoot: a section of Spitfires manoeuvre to attack an enemy formation coming in over the south coast. (Copyright Joe Crowfoot)

They had been promised an easy victory by their high command against an already depleted and demoralized foe, whose finest fighters were no match for their Me 109s. But with the losses mounting in the last few days they knew it was going to be a hard and bloody struggle against a brave and determined enemy. The Spitfire in particular had proved itself equal to the 109 in many individual dogfights.

The frustration among the Germans was illustrated when Göring asked a group of his officers what more they needed to defeat the RAF, at which Adolf Galland asked to be equipped with a squadron of Spitfires. Göring fumed, but Galland was being sarcastic as he strongly believed in the superiority of the Me 109, but was dismayed by the way his pilots were being asked to deploy them in close escort to the bombers.

But Fighter Command's plight was becoming equally stark, as in the previous

One of the Few: Pilot Officer Nigel Rose of No. 602 Squadron, from a painting by David Pritchard. (Courtesy of Nigel Rose)

ten days it had lost 150 pilots. Lord Beaverbrook continued to produce sufficient aircraft to replace those lost in combat, but without trained pilots to fly them the situation was becoming critical.

ANOTHER BAD DAY – 18 AUGUST

If Göring was going to be true to his word and smash Fighter Command in five days, Sunday 18 August was when he expected to finish it. After further reassurance from their leaders that the RAF was already beaten, the Luftwaffe made another massive attempt at winning air supremacy. Little did they know that it would turn out to be yet another bad day.

Around midday huge formations began to home in on the sector stations at Biggin Hill and Kenley. German intelligence had by now realised the importance of these command centres, from which attacks against their own aircraft were orchestrated.

The planned assault on Biggin Hill involved a succession of low-level and high-level raids at five-minute intervals. However, RDF proved its worth again and the Biggin Hill sector commander ordered a Spitfire and two Hurricane squadrons to intercept. Although bombs hit the airfield, German losses were crippling. In one Staffel of nine Stukas, only two would return home.

The attack on Kenley was more successful, with up to 100 bombs hitting the target and six Hurricanes being destroyed on the ground.

In the early afternoon von Sperrle's Luftflotte 3 made attacks on the airfields at Gosport, Thorney Island and Ford. They also attacked Poling RDF station, which was put out of action for ten days. However, during this devastating day the Junkers 87 'Stukas' suffered so heavily that they were withdrawn from the battle and not used again.

This huge Luftwaffe effort had been intended to win air supremacy over southern England in order for the invasion to be launched, yet with the loss of another seventy-one aircraft Göring was far from victorious. Hitler postponed the invasion until 17 September.

5

PHASE THREE – THE BID FOR AIR SUPREMACY

As both sides reflected on the situation on 19 August, it might have seemed to some that the German effort had been cancelled out. Of course it was on the following day that Churchill made his famous speech, which included the words, 'Never in the field of human conflict was so much owed by so many to so few.' Although his speeches often sounded victorious, even when facing possible defeat, he himself would not have believed that the worst was over and certainly Hugh Dowding and Keith Park knew that the enemy was still massed

Hurricanes at a Satellite Airfield During the Battle of Britain by Joe Crowfoot. (Copyright Joe Crowfoot)

in strength and undefeated. Göring might have failed in his first attempt, but in order for an invasion to succeed in mid-September there was still time for one more chance to beat Fighter Command, if he could benefit from a few days of fine weather. German records state that the next stage of the battle began on 19 August, whereas British historians largely accept 24 August as the start date. Both, however, agree that it lasted until 6 September and would include the most precarious phase of the battle for Fighter Command.

LULL BEFORE THE STORM

Poor weather between 19 and 23 August was responsible for a lull in the fighting and gave both sides a chance to rethink their tactics. During these few days of relative quiet there were still numerous attacks on airfields and industrial centres but many of these, whether by day or night, were classed as nuisance raids by small groups or even solitary bombers. This reduced activity can be measured in the low number of enemy aircraft lost; on 19 August there were only six, while

A melee takes place somewhere over the River Thames in the summer of 1940. (Copyright Jonathan Reeve JR2304b102p419391945)

on the next four days there were six, twelve, two and five, respectively. Over the same period the RAF losses were three, two, one, five and nil.

At this point in the battle the city of London had still not been bombed. In fact, attacks on the capital had been expressly forbidden by Hitler himself. To a large extent Glasgow and Liverpool enjoyed a similar immunity, although both were occasionally targeted with Göring's agreement.

CHANGING OF THE OLD GUARD

On 19 August, Göring held a conference at Karinhall at which he told his air corps and geschwader commanders that he was not satisfied with the performance of their fighter pilots. This would have to change and he stressed that the decisive period of the air war against Britain had now been reached. In order to succeed, he told them that he wanted each *geschwader* to be led by young men with a high number of fighter victories. Because of this he ruthlessly replaced many of his existing commanders. For instance, he appointed Adolf Galland commander of JG26 in place of Gotthardt Handrick, who had won a gold medal for the modern pentathlon at the 1936 Olympic Games. At the same time, Galland was decorated with the gold pilot's badge with jewels. Similarly decorated and promoted to command JG51 was Major Werner Mölders, who was regarded as the ultimate role model for all young German boys. He was the first fighter pilot to exceed Baron von Richtofen's eighty victories and the first to reach the 100 mark, his final tally of the war being 115. These were the calibre of men that Göring hoped would inspire his troops and lead them to victory.

Once the decisive battle began, Göring demanded that the destruction of the enemy's fighters should be paramount. 'If they do not take the air', he said, 'we shall attack them on the ground.' Surprise attacks on aircraft factories would also be made both day and night, and secondary targets would be the RAF's bomber stations. The Germans would now almost entirely concentrate their daylight attacks on the south-east corner of England, and there would be a far greater emphasis on destroying the vital sector stations that allowed No. 11 Group to control its squadrons so effectively.

ALL-OUT OFFENSIVE

When the resumed all-out offensive began, German formations would now only contain enough bombers to tempt No. 11 Group into action. Each bomber

Statue of Sir Keith Park in Waterloo Place, London. (Copyright Peter Trimming and licensed for reuse under the Creative Commons Licence)

AIR CHIEF MARSHAL
SIR KEITH PARK
GCB, KBE, MC & BAR, DFC, DCL, MA, RAF
1892 - 1975

formation would be escorted by larger numbers of fighters than previously. Another new tactic would be for aircraft to continuously patrol the Straits of Dover and occasionally make a feint towards the British coast in order to conceal preparations for genuine attacks. This could cause Fighter Command to waste its efforts and resources in scrambling unnecessary sorties.

At the same time Keith Park, almost intuitively, issued orders to his sector controllers that he hoped would counter the enemy's air strategy, some of the crucial points being that they were no longer to position fighters to intercept the enemy over the sea. Instead they would have to stay over land or within gliding distance of it to minimise the number of force-landings in the water and reduce the amount of aircraft lost at sea that might otherwise have been saved if they had come down on the land. Also, they were not to let their fighters chase reconnaissance aircraft or small fighter formations out to sea. From now on, bombers had to be the most important target and fighters should only be engaged when unavoidable. This would prove to be the most difficult order to implement, as under Göring's new strategy the bombers would now be escorted by a great many more Me 109s. Perhaps Park's most telling statement was for controllers to request fighters from Leigh-Mallory's No. 12 Group to protect their airfields while their own squadrons based around London were in the air.

All of these measures seem to read Göring's mind, particularly the fact that during the coming phase No. 11 Group was going to bear almost the whole of the Luftwaffe's strength. Further evidence of this happened on Thursday 22 August when Göring ordered von Sperrle to put all of Luftflotte 3's fighter aircraft under the command of Kesselring's Luftflotte 2. They were subsequently ordered to move from the Cherbourg area, from where they had hitherto attacked the south and south-west of England, to the Pas de Calais, for attacks on the south-east and potentially London itself, if and when the Führer was ready to give the order. To compensate for this loss Stumpff, who had no Me 109 short-range fighters serving in Luftflotte 5, was instructed to send all his long-range Me 110 fighters to Luftflotte 3. This meant that, although his air fleet would no longer take part in any major daylight offensives against the north of Britain, when his aircraft took part in night-time raids they would be totally without fighter support.

A NEW OFFENSIVE BEGINS

On Saturday 24 August the Luftwaffe launched the next and most dangerous phase of the battle, and its second bid for air superiority. During the day, what were regarded as crucial airfields to the British effort became the targets, with heavy raids against North Weald, Hornchurch and most particularly Manston, where the damage was so severe to the buildings and runways that it had to be evacuated and abandoned as a fighter station. A large formation was encountered by No. 65 Squadron at around 1530 hours, at 22,000ft over Dover.

During the night of 24 August, 170 raiders attacked targets in northern and south-east England. Once again, the escalation in the level of violence can be measured in aircraft lost: twenty-two for the RAF and thirty-eight for the Luftwaffe. This was just the start of the new offensive, and between now and 6 September the Germans carried out an average of 1,000 individual sorties per day. On 30 and 31 August, more than 1,600 came over. Yet the average number of bombers was only 250 a day, which illustrates the formation balances during this new fighter-intensive strategy. Faced with this overwhelming and determined

The main operations room at RAF Uxbridge, from where Keith Park directed the fight in the south-east. This would prove to be the nerve centre of the entire battle. (Copyright Anguskirk and licensed for reuse under the Creative Commons Licence)

escort force, No. 11 Group would find it hard to deal with the bombers from the very onset. True, they would exact a heavy toll on the German fighters, but Fighter Command would also begin to lose more pilots and aircraft than they could afford. Soon the situation would become deadly serious.

London Bombed Against Hitler's Orders

It was during the evening of 24 August that an event took place that would have a profound effect on the final outcome of the battle, although not immediately so. Bombs intended for oil refineries at Thames Haven and aircraft factories at Rochester and Kingston were jettisoned mistakenly over central London by crews who appear to have had only a vague notion of their whereabouts. This, of course, was still prohibited by German high command. The following day, all German bomber units received a telegram from Göring demanding to know the names of captains whose crews had dropped bombs within the London perimeter. Those responsible would be posted to serve in infantry regiments.

The Reichsmarschall rightly feared reprisals as he had publicly boasted that bombs would never fall on Berlin. He had reason to be concerned because on the night of Sunday 25 August, Bomber Command sent a force of eighty-one Hampdens to attack the Siemens-Halske factory and other targets in and around Berlin. Some of their bombs landed on the city itself. The capital may have suffered damage, but Göring himself would suffer further damming ridicule among the German people and his own staff. This action had shown in no uncertain terms that if the Luftwaffe failed to win the Battle of Britain, their failure could ultimately lead to an air battle over Germany itself.

This incident aside, the Luftwaffe kept up the pressure on Fighter Command with attacks during the day on Warmwell airfield and targets in the west of England. There were also heavy raids on Dover, the Thames Estuary and Pembroke docks. During the night there were widespread raids throughout England, Scotland and Wales.

Cooperation Between Groups

On Monday 26 August the pace continued relentlessly. At 1100 hours, over 150 hostiles attacked Biggin Hill and Kenley; they also bombed Folkestone and set

Bristol Blenheim night fighter of No. 604 Squadron flying from Middle Wallop during the summer of 1940. (Courtesy of Severnside Aviation Society)

fire to the balloon barrage at Dover. In the afternoon another 100-plus made for Hornchurch and North Weald, but were largely driven off. They did, however, manage to cause severe damage to the airfield at Debden. On this particular day Keith Park had asked for fighters from Leigh-Mallory and No. 12 Group to guard Debden while his own aircraft were airborne. Although they did eventually arrive, it was too late to see any action. This was to further damage the strained relations that existed between Park and Leigh-Mallory, who at the full height of the battle seem to have had a running feud, both highly critical of the other.

If Keith Park found his squadrons overstretched he would seek reinforcements from the two groups that flanked him, No. 10 Group to the west and No. 12 Group to the north. If he did this it was usually to ask for fighters to patrol and protect his airfields while his own fighters tackled the enemy. This was to help reduce damage to his stations so that his squadrons would have somewhere to return after each engagement. Park found Brand's fighters extremely helpful and willing to oblige, but with Leigh-Mallory it was a different story. He would appear to have had something of a chip on his shoulder. The way he saw it, Keith Park was getting all the action and glory, and he was determined that his own squadrons would play a leading role in the battle, and not merely support No. 11 Group. Park, probably with good cause, complained to Dowding that Leigh-Mallory's squadrons hardly ever went where they were asked and were always popping up in places where his controllers had no means of keeping track of them. Consequently, his airfields were taking an unnecessary pounding.

On Thursday 29 August the commander of Kesselring's fighter organisation, General Kurt von Doring, claimed that the Luftwaffe had won unlimited fighter superiority over England. Although Fighter Command was on the back heel, they were still fighting successfully. Doring's rather rash claim encouraged Hitler to announce that the invasion fleet would sail on 20 September and troops would land in England the next day.

NIGHT INTERCEPTION

In August 1940 airborne radar was still very much in its infancy, but something had to be done about the German raiders coming across the coast at night. The Germans had a fantastic radio navigation system code-named 'Knickebein' which enabled them to find their targets in the dark. With only a few dedicated night fighter Blenheim squadrons with experimental radar units to cover the whole of

After the Sortie by Joe Crowfoot. A Spitfire and its pilot arrive safely back at a grass airfield from a mission. (Copyright Joe Crowfoot)

Britain, Fighter Command had little option but to use the aircraft they had available to them as best they could. At the start of the battle this included Hurricanes and Spitfires; in fact, all fighter pilots would have undergone night interception training.

For this purpose, squadrons in the line would always have a few fighters on night readiness. Once the RDF chain had detected a possible hostile aircraft, the sector control room would notify the appropriate squadron to scramble its night fighters. Then, using the RDF and possible Observer Corps tracks, the controller would have to try and direct the fighters towards the enemy bomber until they were able to see it. At night this was the most difficult part of the operation. But even on the darkest night there were clues to the aircraft's whereabouts, such as the glow from the engines. A fighter pilot might get lucky if the bomber had been illuminated by searchlights. However, in this eventuality it usually meant that an anti-aircraft battery would already be firing at the intruder. In order for the Spitfire or Hurricane to avoid being hit by the anti-aircraft fire itself they were fitted with a downward recognition light which the pilot could signal for the ground guns to disengage. Another problem was of course the journey back to the fighter station, bearing in mind that the pilot was unable to see the ground beneath him, so once again it was down to the controller to guide him home.

FIGHTER COMMAND AT BREAKING POINT

The next significant occurrence during the battle took place on Friday 30 August, which was the start of an even more intense period of attacks against airfields and RDF stations that stretched Fighter Command almost to breaking point. The weather on the day was fine and in the morning ships were attacked in the Thames Estuary as a diversion designed to lure the British fighters away from the Luftwaffe's real purpose of the day: a sustained assault against their enemy. This would involve attacks on Biggin Hill, Kenley, Tangmere, North Weald and Shoreham, as well as the RDF stations at Rye, Pevensey, Foreness, Dover, Fairlight, Beachy Head and Whitstable. The Vauxhall factory at Luton, the Coastal Command airfield at Detling and Oxford were also badly hit. During the evening and night, bombers continued their nocturnal blitz of towns and cities, particularly those with a relevant industrial base, with Liverpool, Derby, Norwich and Peterborough all targeted. The vital sector station at Biggin Hill, which guarded the southern approaches to London, was hit three times in the day, the second being an accurate and devastating attack. To achieve all of this the Luftwaffe spent another thirty-six aircraft for the RAF's twenty-five.

For the first time in the battle, Fighter Command flew more than a thousand sorties in a day. German intelligence had convinced Göring that Dowding was down to his last few fighters, yet his formations were met by greater numbers of Spitfires and Hurricanes than ever before, or so it seemed. Of course, things were beginning to get critical for Keith Park, who would have every available aircraft in the air. One of the main reasons for this was that they were safer in the sky than as sitting ducks on an airfield.

The German pilots had once again been led to believe that the RAF was all but finished, yet here they were inflicting deadly retribution and seemingly as strong as ever. Having said that, because of the Luftwaffe's numerically superior fighter escorts the RAF pilots found it difficult to get in among the bombers and prevent their cargo from hitting their airfields.

BIGGIN HILL FEELS THE STRAIN

On Saturday 31 August, Kesselring mounted another day of heavy attacks on No. 11 Group's airfields, his targets this time being Debden, Hornchurch, Croydon,

Detling, North Weald and Biggin Hill. Some of these, particularly Debden and Biggin Hill, were hit extremely badly, the latter losing its operations block. This was a crippling blow for Park, as damage to several other airfields such as Manston, West Malling, Lympne and Hawkinge had already made them almost unusable. He was running out of aerodromes from which to carry on an adequate defence of London and if the onslaught continued he might have to withdraw all of his force to airfields north of the Thames, which would effectively gift Göring his much desired air supremacy over Kent. There were three squadrons based at Biggin Hill, two of which he had no choice but to relocate, while the third was temporarily controlled from a shop in the nearby village until a more suitable arrangement could be made.

Also on 31 August Kesselring sent a raid against Duxford, which of course was within No. 12 Group's area of control; between them No. 111 Squadron and No. 19 Squadron managed to force the raiders away, who largely jettisoned their bombs over the Essex countryside. The Coastal Command station at Eastchurch was also singled out for attention once more, as were the RDF sites at Pevensey, Rye, Beachy Head, Whitstable, and Foreness. During the night there were widespread attacks on numerous targets.

This had been a difficult day for Fighter Command, and if the rest of Park's airfields were put out of action and Göring could keep up this level of intensity he could well achieve air superiority over the south-east in a matter of days. However, Göring did not seem to grasp the fact that if he concentrated solely on the sector airfields such as Biggin Hill, Tangmere and Kenley, Dowding might well have been staring defeat in the face. Instead, he continued to attack a diverse range of targets, many of which were aircraft factories; in a sense this was pointless, because if he had won air superiority and the invasion had begun, the aircraft these factories were manufacturing would never have reached Fighter Command in time anyway. This was the breaking point, and if German high command had really appreciated how grave the situation was for Fighter Command, this was the point at which they could have finished things off.

The Battle of Britain Memorial Flight pictured at Duxford in 2004, here comprised of two Spitfires and a Lancaster bomber. (Copyright Airwolfhound and licensed for reuse under the Creative Commons Licence)

INTO SEPTEMBER

The first six days of September followed a similar pattern, with attacks on airfields by day, while at night the bombers mainly sought out the aircraft factories. Sunday 1 September was another fine day and there were attacks on the airfields at Eastchurch, Detling, Lympne, and Hawkinge. Biggin Hill received another pounding. That night Göring sought to destroy factories with relevance to the aircraft industry in Sheffield, Stafford, Liverpool, Hull, Grimsby, Burton and South Wales.

On Monday 2 September there would be further daylight attacks on airfields with Biggin Hill, Rochford, Debden, North Weald, Eastchurch, Kenley, Hornchurch, Detling and Digby all targeted. The aircraft factory at Brooklands was also raided. That night, Liverpool and Birmingham took the main punishment during a day of high losses on both sides, with the RAF losing thirty-one and the Luftwaffe thirty-five.

THE PRESSURE MOUNTS ON FIGHTER COMMAND

Tuesday 3 September saw further airfield attacks, with Hornchurch, North Weald and Debden all damaged. That night, Liverpool, South Wales and the south-east were raided and the RAF and Luftwaffe lost sixteen aircraft each.

With fine weather on the following day, Thursday September 5, there was still no respite for Fighter Command, as it sustained another series of devastating attacks, this time with Croydon itself among airfields to feel the heat. There were also raids on North Weald, Lympne, Eastchurch, and Hornchurch. Biggin Hill took another pounding, although it was already by now all but closed to the RAF. During the night there were another series of attacks, mainly around Liverpool, Manchester and the London periphery. Once again, Keith Park requested the help of Leigh-Mallory's No. 12 Group to help protect his airfields while his own squadrons were dealing with the bombers.

Although the weather on Friday 6 September remained fine, the Luftwaffe's activity was scaled down for the day, with only Biggin Hill and the aircraft factory at Brooklands being targeted by day, followed by light raids on several places during the night. It was another case of the lull before the storm as many of Göring's aerial troops prepared for the next phase of the battle, which, unsuspected by Hugh Dowding and his group commanders, was due to begin on the following day. Having said that, there were still many aircraft lost in both camps, with the Luftwaffe losing thirty-five and the RAF twenty-three.

Since August 30 and the start of this latest all-out attempt to win air supremacy and destroy Fighter Command both in the air and on the ground, Göring had heavily attacked Dowding's airfields on eight consecutive days. He had boasted that he would only need five, yet Keith Park and his neighbouring group commanders still managed to deal with most of the raids sent against them. Amazingly, in spite of being on the receiving end of these relentless attacks, the morale of the beleaguered British pilots remained high, even though their ranks were growing thinner by the day. By contrast, the German morale was at rock bottom, the main cause of which being Göring's constant recrimination and blaming of the pilots for his own tactical shortcomings. What also has to be remembered is that although the defenders were beginning to run low on pilots and aircraft, so were the Germans. Since the start of the battle almost two months before, they had lost over 800 aircraft. Their losses could not be replaced that quickly, and although they had done a huge amount of damage to Fighter Command's infrastructure, they would soon be unable to mount raids of the same intensity or with the quantities of aeroplanes involved. Time was running out for both sides and victory hung in the balance.

Saluting the Victor by Joe Crowfoot. A Spitfire of No. 64 Squadron turns for home after a victorious engagement. (Copyright Joe Crowfoot)

6

PHASE FOUR – THEIR FINEST HOUR

On Saturday 7 September 1940, at the very point when their attacks on Dowding's airfields were threatening to become a decisive advantage for the Germans, they made a tactical switch that was of such importance that most people agree it was the turning point of the battle. For some reason, they turned their attention away from attacking Fighter Command to pursue a massive bombing campaign on the city of London. This was the start of the fourth and final phase of the battle.

WHY THE CHANGE OF TACTICS?

There were probably a number of reasons why the Germans decided to make this change and the most urgent of these was undoubtedly the weather. Before long, the inevitability of poor weather conditions as winter approached in the English Channel would make a crossing suicidal without having won air supremacy first. They would therefore have to postpone their efforts until the following spring, by which time both Hitler and Göring knew that Britain would be in a much stronger position to defend itself.

Then again, it was possible the Germans thought that they had already put Fighter Command out of effective action because of all the attacks they had made on its airfields and because of all the RAF aircraft their intelligence gatherers insisted they had destroyed. So perhaps they considered the job had been done and Fighter Command was defeated.

Others argued that an attack on the social and political heart of the country might still force the British government into capitulation. The Blitz on London was also said to reflect the Führer's wishes to carry out concentrated attacks on the city as a reprisal for Bomber Command's daring raid on Berlin on 25 August.

The Chase by Joe Crowfoot. A Hurricane of No. 501 Squadron in pursuit of a Heinkel He 111. (Copyright Joe Crowfoot)

BEGINNING OF THE LONDON BLITZ – 7 SEPTEMBER

Shortly before 1600 hours on 7 September, the formations of enemy aircraft being detected on the other side of the English Channel by the RDF chain were still no indication that the biggest raid of the battle so far was about to be launched.

Because of the importance of the occasion, Göring had taken personal command of the Luftwaffe. He had been involved throughout the planning of this new offensive and wanted to see it through to a satisfactory conclusion. Göring had travelled to the Pas de Calais in his private train and proceeded to watch from the clifftops on Cap Gris Nez opposite Dover, within sight of the English coast, as his aerial armada of nearly 350 bombers and 617 fighters set course for England and headed out across the water.

On the British side of the Channel sector controllers scrambled twenty-one squadrons in defence. Keith Park was himself absent that day but his subordinates at Uxbridge were still expecting No. 11 Group's airfields to be the focus of the raid, and positioned the defending fighters to guard sector stations and other probable targets such as the Thames Haven oil refineries or the aircraft factory at Brooklands. By the time the controllers realised that the bombers were actually heading for London, it was too late and bombs were raining down on the city, mostly around the dockland area from Rotherhithe to Tower Bridge.

The Do 17s of KG2, led by Oberst Johannes Fink, were the vanguard. The few RAF fighters that did arrive on the scene before the enemy turned for home found it almost impossible to make contact with the bombers because of the abundance

CODEWORD 'CROMWELL'

The job of repelling the invasion, if it came, belonged to the Home Forces under the command of General Sir Alan Brooke. As well as British and Commonwealth troops, he would rely on the Home Guard to make up numbers. All of them knew that on receipt of the signal 'Cromwell' the invasion could be expected at any moment. As a complete coincidence, it was on 7 September that the codeword was issued.

Using reconnaissance photographs, British Intelligence had noted a sharp build-up of barges in French ports such as Dunkirk and Calais. They also noted that Kesselring had concentrated all of his dive-bombers near the Straits of Dover. These could be used ahead of the barges to prepare the way for the invasion force. All of this convinced the chiefs of staff that the invasion was about to kick off. They of course had no way of knowing that Hitler had confirmed September 20 as the invasion date.

General Brooke himself was absent that day, but one of his senior officers, Brigadier John Swayne, took it upon himself to issue the signal based on the intelligence provided to him. He therefore issued the signal from GHQ at 2007 and the nation held its breath.

Troops all over the south of England were mobilised, and members of the Home Guard said goodbye to their families and took up their defensive positions. Twelve hours later they were stood down again, somewhat annoyed that the order had been given before the German fleet had actually set sail.

of their Me 109 escorts. The raid was a success for the Luftwaffe, who left huge roaring infernos in their wake and the sky above the city blackened by smoke.

Later that evening, at around 2000 hours, the bombers returned with a vengeance, guided up the Thames Estuary by the glow of burning buildings as they compounded the city's ordeal for a further eight hours. But September 7 was only the beginning of the Blitz on London, which would continue every night without a break and often during the day until 14 November when Coventry was heavily attacked instead, by which time the battle was already officially over.

His Majesty King George VI had expressed a wish that Sunday 8 September should be observed as a special national day of prayer. There was a tremendous response all around the country as people from all backgrounds and walks of life prayed to be saved from invasion and for those fighting for the freedom of their land. The King's call to Britain led to churches being filled to overflowing and many people praying outside on the streets. At a crowded service in Westminster Abbey, the final prayer began, 'Remember, O God, for good, these watchmen, who by day and by night climb into the air. Let thy hand lead them, we beseech thee, and thy right hand hold them.'

FIGHTER COMMAND REBUILDS

In this detail from the stained glass window at St George's Chapel of Remembrance at RAF Biggin Hill, ground crew are servicing an aircraft and making it ready to fly in the battle again. (Copyright Loco Steve and licensed for reuse under the Creative Commons Licence)

Over the next few days, the Blitz on London intensified, with Kesselring bombing by day and von Sperrle by night. However, they were never again able to achieve quite the success of the opening day, as they had lost the element of surprise and Keith Park was able to predict their intentions.

For the country as a whole, the Blitz was a dark and dangerous period, but for Fighter Command there was a positive side. While the Luftwaffe concentrated its attacks on the city, Keith Park's airfields and sector stations could be repaired without fear of attack. They now had the opportunity to slowly recover from the hammering they had taken at the start of the month.

On 1 July 1940, the Prime Minister Winston Churchill had made another of his famous wartime speeches following the withdrawal of the British Expeditionary Force from France and Belgium. The speech included the words,

> The Battle of France is over... the Battle of Britain is about to begin. The whole fury and might of the enemy must soon be turned on us. Hitler knows that he will have to break us in this island or lose the war ... let us therefore brace ourselves to our duties, and so bear ourselves that, if the Empire and its Commonwealth last for a thousand years, men will say, 'This was their finest hour.'

Two and a half months later, after inexhaustibly repelling everything that the Luftwaffe could throw at them by both day and night, the surviving aircrew of Fighter Command, the 'Few,' were about to become immortally and indelibly linked to these words. They were about to prove to the entire world, and the subsequent history of humanity, that what happened next would indeed be their finest hour.

BATTLE OF BRITAIN DAY – 15 SEPTEMBER

Sunday 15 September 1940 was the day that the Battle of Britain was finally won and lost. The Germans made two massive raids on London, designed to attract every remaining RAF fighter into the fray. Once again, the enemy had been told by their leaders that Fighter Command was finished. The invasion fleet was assembled and waited for the signal to arrive that air supremacy was complete.

It so happened that Winston Churchill had famously chosen to visit RAF Uxbridge that day and watched the whole thing unfold on the plotting table from the gallery. At one point he turned to Keith Park and asked him what reserves he had left. Park had to admit, 'None!'

The leader of the Duxford Wing, Squadron Leader Douglas Bader (centre), is pictured here with Flight Lieutenant G. Ball DFC and Pilot Officer W. McKnight DFC. Ball, who was British, and McKnight, who was Canadian, both served with Bader's 242 Squadron, and both were killed in the battle. (Courtesy of Michael Virtue, Virtue Books)

The first raiders began to assemble over the French coast at around 1030 in the morning. RDF tracked their every move. Park scrambled eleven of his twenty-one single-seat squadrons; others would join in later. At the same time Quintin Brand dispatched a squadron from Middle Wallop in No. 10 Group and Leigh-Mallory sent off the Duxford Wing from No. 12 Group.

THE BIG WING

One of the most controversial aspects of the RAF's defence of Britain was the Duxford or 'Big' Wing, commanded and led by Squadron Leader Douglas Bader. At full strength, this comprised three Hurricane and two Spitfire squadrons. The idea behind the wing was to meet the enemy in force. Once vectored on to a group of raiders, the terrifying sight of potentially sixty fighters closing in for the kill was intended to disrupt the enemy, causing them to scatter.

The Germans crossed the coast near Dover and now had to run the gauntlet posed by the formidable array of defending fighters. The RAF pilots fought with such passion that the formations were quickly dispersed. Those that did manage to press on through No. 11 Group's fighter screen suddenly found themselves facing Bader's Big Wing. Their hearts must surely have sunk at the sight that met their eyes. Far from being finished, as their generals had promised them, the RAF was still able to field substantial formations.

The Duxford Wing had its critics, most notably Keith Park himself, who maintained that they always arrived late, and only after his own units had done all the hard work. But on 15 September they proved their worth and helped to tip the balance in favour of Fighter Command.

By mid-day the raid had petered out and the Germans returned to their bases so they could prepare to take part in the afternoon operation. In the few hours it took them to regroup, Dowding's aircraft had been refuelled and rearmed. Many of the pilots had also eaten a meal and rested. As the tired, disillusioned German aircrews began to form up again at around 1400 hours, their RAF counterparts were refreshed and waiting for them.

The Battle of Britain Memorial, which is sited on the white cliffs at Capel-le-Ferne near Folkestone. (Copyright Helmut Zozmann and licensed for reuse under the Creative Commons Licence)

Keith Park pre-empted their ploy and sent up twelve squadrons before they had even reached the English coast. Once again, Brand sent reinforcements on the left and Leigh-Mallory dispatched the Duxford Wing.

THE GREAT FIGHTER BATTLE

Throwing caution to the wind, Kesselring decided to send a large part of his remaining fighter force ahead of the bombers to sweep the RAF out of the sky over London, which would give them a clear run to the capital.

When the German advance guard at last reached the city, they found no fewer than fifteen Spitfire and Hurricane squadrons waiting for them.

It was during the next half-hour on the afternoon of 15 September that the real Battle of Britain took place, as two armies of opposing fighter aircraft met for the first time in substantial numbers. Now, at last, Kesselring had the opportunity of sweeping Fighter Command aside and winning control of the skies.

Wimpeys by Joe Crowfoot. The Vickers Wellington was Bomber Command's main day bomber at the time of the battle, attacking targets such as the barge concentrations that were being readied for the invasion of England. (Copyright Joe Crowfoot)

As the fighter battle ebbed and flowed, the bombers arrived in its wake and dropped huge bomb loads on to the burning city below. But as they did so, Douglas Bader and the Duxford Wing appeared on the horizon. They separated, announced their 'tally-hos' and went ruthlessly in for the kill, pursuing their quarry relentlessly and with little mercy.

It must have appeared to the battle-weary Germans that not only had they been unable to achieve air supremacy on this pivotal day, but the likelihood of them ever securing it seemed more remote than ever. After weeks and weeks of attrition, Fighter Command still had the ability to send up hundreds of fighter aircraft against every raid they launched.

In terms of German losses, these are hard to confirm as every account you read is different. The most likely figure is fifty-six destroyed.

In the summer of 1940, in fear that the Nazis were about to invade Britain, defences were hurriedly built all along the coast and inland on what became known as stop lines. After Hitler cancelled the invasion these defences were largely abandoned, and now, like the pillbox on a Somerset beach seen in this picture, they are a reminder of the dark days of the Battle of Britain. (Copyright Henry Buckton)

HITLER CANCELS THE INVASION OF BRITAIN

The following day the Luftwaffe licked its wounds and tried to come to terms with what had happened. The morale of the pilots had been completely shattered and they no longer had enough aircraft left to carry out many further large-scale daylight raids.

On 18 September General Jodl had the unenviable task of explaining to the Führer that his invasion fleet, which was gathered in the Channel ports, was being systematically destroyed almost to annihilation by RAF Bomber Command, RAF Coastal Command and Royal Navy bombardment. Hitler had no choice but to abandon his plans to invade Britain. All the troops that had been gathering to take part in Operation Sealion were withdrawn, never to re-assemble.

Although not technically part of the Battle of Britain, which was fought specifically between the Luftwaffe and Fighter Command, the campaign by the RAF to prevent an invasion by bombing Hitler's invasion infrastructure ran concurrently with the former and certainly deserves a mention. As the threat of invasion became more acute in the early part of July, high priority was given to attacking German ports, shipping and, in particular, invasion barges. When it became known that large quantities of barges were moving towards the Channel ports, as well as an armada of naval vessels and requisitioned fishing trawlers, Air Chief-Marshal Portal, the commander-in-chief of Bomber Command, began a process of bombing these concentrations at night, as well as keeping up the pressure on inland targets that were helping to sustain Germany's war effort.

LUFTWAFFE TACTICS IN THE FACE OF DEFEAT

Although the Battle of Britain had been won, the war still went on and the Germans had no choice but to keep up the pressure on Britain by blockading her by sea and air. From now on the Luftwaffe's main strategy was to attack London and other major cities during the night, when the bombers could be deployed without fighter protection.

This gave Göring the problem of what to do with his now redundant Messerschmitts, so to keep them occupied he had them converted into what were known as fighter-bombers, which carried small bomb loads. Thus armed, these began to raid southern England in small numbers, popping up anywhere and everywhere, often unannounced by radar. These 'tip-and-run' raids caused varying degrees of damage, but certainly kept Fighter Command on its toes.

For what remained of the battle, Göring's tactics would change little; the

ITALY ENTERS THE FRAY

On 4 October, Hitler met with Mussolini and, although the Führer gave him little encouragement, the Italian dictator must have felt that the battle was still winnable. Not wanting to miss out on the glory, he decided to send units of his own air force, the Regia Aeronautica Italiana, to Belgium, where they were under the command of Luftflotte 2. This Italian air contingent was equipped with around eighty Fiat BR20s; fifty Fiat CR42s; and forty-eight Fiat G50s. The BR20 was an all-metal medium bomber, whereas the CR42 and G50 were both fighters.

The BR20 Cicogna, or 'Stork', was powered with two Fiat A80 radial engines and had a maximum speed of 255 mph. When carrying a crew of five and a bomb-load of one ton, it had a range of around 1,350 miles. It was armed with three machine-guns.

The CR42 Freccia, or 'Arrow', was powered by a Fiat A74 radial engine. It was a single-seat biplane fighter that must have seemed terribly old-fashioned to its British foe. Carrying only two machine-guns and with a maximum speed of 270 mph, it seemed almost pitiful against the RAF's monoplane fighters. Although the G50 Falco, or 'Falcon', was a monoplane and had four machine-guns, it still could only manage a top speed of 290 mph, so it was also massively out-performed by the British fighters it encountered.

On Friday 25 October, sixteen Italian Fiat BR20 Cicogna bombers joined a night raid on the port of Harwich. Then, on Tuesday 29 October, fifteen bombers escorted by around seventy Fiat CR42s attempted a bombing raid on Ramsgate, but as soon as the formation was engaged by anti-aircraft fire it turned back. These aircraft were not identified by the British as being Italian at the time, and the truth only came out after the battle was over. Although the Italians continued to operate during the night-time raids in the future, these were their only minor contributions to the Battle of Britain itself.

fighter-bombers continued to harass a diverse range of targets by day, while London was pounded at night. One of his intentions was to smash the morale of the civilian population of the country, but of course, as history has shown, instead they rallied behind their leaders and the war effort. People everywhere dug for victory, queued for their rations, and whistled while they worked. Churchill's broadcasts to the nation galvanized them into being more united in purpose than at any other time in history, before or since.

The period historians attribute to the Battle of Britain lasted until 31 October 1940, and surprisingly there was still one last twist in the tale.

BACK TO SQUARE ONE

At the start of November the Germans made a dramatic shift back to attacking shipping in the Thames Estuary and convoys in the English Channel. As far as the Luftwaffe was concerned, their tactics would revert back to the same as those they had employed during the first phase of the battle in early July. Blockade was once again the order of the day. To find themselves back to square one, having gained no ground or tactical advantage after four months of fighting, during which the elite of Germany's young flyers had been killed, maimed or taken prisoner, must

The medals of Pilot Officer Kenneth Graham Hart, with the DFC on the left. Perhaps of more interest is the rare Battle of Britain clasp on the ribbon of the 1939/45 Star. (Courtesy of Simon Muggleton)

Detail from the Battle of Britain Memorial on London's Embankment. (Copyright Henry Buckton)

have been unbelievably devastating for the survivors.

In terms of aircraft losses during the whole period, the accepted figures are 915 for Fighter Command and 1,733 for the Luftwaffe.

As for the 'Few', those who had administered the first defeat to Nazi Germany, there was little time for celebration, as the war had to go on. There were new campaigns to win if the world was to be free of evil.

THE IMPORTANCE OF BRITAIN'S VICTORY IN THE BATTLE

Because of the Battle of Britain, the country remained unoccupied and provided a springboard for attacks against the aggressors. If Britain had succumbed to the Nazi jackboot in 1940, it is very unlikely that America would have become embroiled in a European war. So there would have been no subsequent success in the Battle of the Atlantic, no victory in the western desert, no D-Day, no liberation of occupied lands, and, perhaps most chilling of all, the Nazis would unquestionably have developed nuclear weapons, the consequences of which are unimaginable.

If Britain had been invaded in 1940, it might still be a very different place today. It might not be the colourful, multi-cultural and tolerant society it has since become. So every one of us in these islands and indeed throughout much of Europe is indebted to the men and women who secured that first victory over the Nazis. We are indebted to each one of these for bestowing on us a gift that we hardly know we have – our freedom.

WHAT NEXT?

TV

Battle of Britain: The Real Story (2010)
Battle of Britain: The South Coast Trail (2010)
Finest Hour (1999)
First Light (2010)
Piece of Cake (1988)
Spitfire Women (2010)

FILMS

Angels One Five (1952)
Battle of Britain (1969)
The First of the Few (1942)
Hope and Glory (1987)
Reach for the Sky (1956)

NOVELS AND FICTION

Jackson, Robert, *The Battle of Britain: a Novel of 1940*
Olsen, David, *Dragon Flight*
Olsen, David, *Spitfire Sunrise*
Robinson, Derek, *Piece of Cake*
Schrader, Helena, *Where Eagles Never Flew*

NON-FICTION

Bishop, Patrick, *Fighter Boys: Saving Britain 1940*
Buckton, Henry, *Voices from The Battle of Britain*
Deighton, Len, *Battle of Britain*
Deighton, Len, *Fighter*
Flint, Peter, *Dowding and Headquarters Fighter Command*
Hillary, Richard, *The Last Enemy*
Neil, Tom, *Gun Button to Fire*
Orange, Vincent, *Sir Keith Park*
Price, Alfred, *The Hardest Day 18 August 1940*
Ramsey, Winston, *The Battle of Britain: Then and Now*
Ramsey, Winston, *The Blitz: Then and Now*
Townsend, Peter, *Duel of Eagles*
Turner, John Frayn, *Battle of Britain*
Wood, Derek, and Dempster, Derek, *The Narrow Margin*
Wynn, Kenneth, *Men of the Battle of Britain*

INDEX

Also in the Illustrated Introductions series

Fascinated by history? Wish you knew more?
The Illustrated Introductions are here to help.

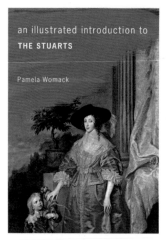

An Illustrated Introduction
to the Stuarts

978-1-4456-3788-4

£9.99

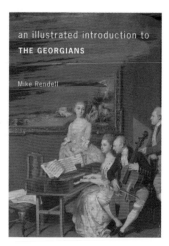

An Illustrated Introduction
to the Georgians

978-1-4456-3630-6

£9.99

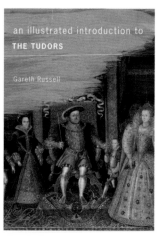

An Illustrated Introduction
to the Tudors

978-1-4456-4121-8

£9.99

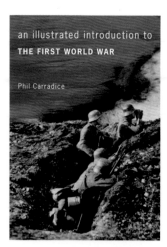

An Illustrated Introduction
to the First World War

978-1-4456-3296-4

£9.99

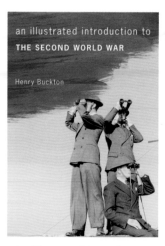

An Illustrated Introduction
to the Second World War

978-1-4456-3848-5

£9.99

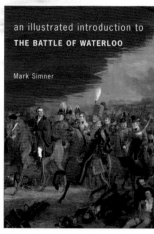

An Illustrated Introduction
to the Battle of Waterloo

978-1-4456-4666 4

£9.99

Available from all good bookshops or to order direct
Please call **01453-847-800**
www.amberley-books.com